UNRELENTING PRAYER

BOB SORGE

†

OASIS HOUSE

Fourth Printing (2013)

Other books by Bob Sorge:

- BETWEEN THE LINES: God Is Writing Your Story
- MINUTE MEDITATIONS
- OPENED FROM THE INSIDE: Taking the Stronghold of Zion
- POWER OF THE BLOOD
- IT'S NOT BUSINESS, IT'S PERSONAL
- LOYALTY: The Reach Of The Noble Heart
- FOLLOWING THE RIVER: A Vision For Corporate Worship
- ENVY: The Enemy Within
- SECRETS OF THE SECRET PLACE
- Secrets of the Secret Place COMPANION STUDY GUIDE
- Secrets of the Secret Place LEADER'S MANUAL
- GLORY: When Heaven Invades Earth
- DEALING WITH THE REJECTION AND PRAISE OF MAN
- PAIN, PERPLEXITY, AND PROMOTION: A prophetic interpretation of the book of Job
- THE FIRE OF GOD'S LOVE
- THE FIRE OF DELAYED ANSWERS
- IN HIS FACE: A prophetic call to renewed focus
- EXPLORING WORSHIP: A practical guide to praise and worship
- Exploring Worship WORKBOOK & DISCUSSION GUIDE

UNRELENTING PRAYER
Copyright © 2005 by Bob Sorge
Published by Oasis House
P.O. Box 522
Grandview, Missouri 64030-0522
www.oasishouse.com

All Scripture quotations are from the New King James Version of the Bible. Copyright © 1979, 1980, 1982, Thomas Nelson Inc., Publisher. Used by permission.

Edited by Edie Veach.

Printed in the United States of America
ISBN-10: 0-9704791-3-6
ISBN 13: 978-0-9704791-3-4
Library of Congress Cataloging-in-Publication Data

Sorge, Bob.
  Unrelenting prayer / Bob Sorge.
      p. cm.
  Includes bibliographical references.
  ISBN 978-0-9704791-3-4 (alk. paper)
  1. Prayer–Christianity. 2. Prayer–Biblical teaching. 3. Unjust judge (Parable) 4. Bible. N.T. Luke XVIII, 1-8–Theology. I. Title.
  BV220.S69 2005
  248.3'2–dc22
                              2005024071

DEDICATION

I dedicate this book to our spiritual family here in Kansas City, the International House Of Prayer—and more than that, to the 24/7 prayer movement that is spreading throughout the earth. We are rediscovering our corporate identity to truly be, as Jesus Himself put it, "a house of prayer" (Matthew 21:13). This prayer/worship movement is a sign in itself that the return of Jesus is drawing near.

Never before has the church cried out so vociferously and insistently for spiritual breakthrough. We are desperate for apostolic Christianity in our generation, and believe that the incessant prayers of the church are the only way forward. My purpose in writing this book is to fuel the fires of the praying church. May the body of Christ be equipped and empowered to lift unrelenting, lovesick cries to our Beloved until He rends the heavens (Isaiah 64:1) and visits us with His glory and power.

Bob Sorge
Kansas City, Missouri
September, 2005

CONTENTS

FOREWORD

I believe we are living in the generation in which the Lord returns. At the top of the Holy Spirit's agenda in this final hour is the mobilization of a worldwide prayer and worship movement. Jesus will not return to earth in a vacuum but only by the beckoning of a praying church. The Father sent Jesus the first time in answer to the prayers of people like Anna and Simeon. Just as God called Anna to fast and pray night and day for over 60 years (Luke 2:36-38), we are asking God to raise up a million Annas who will cry out night and day until Christ's Second Coming.

Since September 1999, I have had the privilege of directing a 24/7 nonstop prayer ministry. We have 84 two-hour prayer meetings a week, each led by worship teams. At the International House of Prayer of Kansas City, I am watching men and women of all ages—from children to young adults to the elderly—abandon themselves to keeping charge of the Lord's sanctuary through prayer and worship. God is raising up an army who will not give the

Lord rest, but are crying out day and night to Him until He makes His people a praise in the earth. I promise you—their cries will be heard and their prayers answered.

May God raise up thousands of forerunners who will trumpet the Spirit's call to day and night prayer. This book is one such clarion call. Bob Sorge is qualified to write on this subject. His entire family jumped in at ground level to help build the International House of Prayer. His wife, Marci, is one of our senior leaders, and his children serve on worship teams and in various leadership capacities. The entire Sorge family is deeply invested in the truths presented in this book. We don't need more books on prayer that come from a theoretical perspective, or that focus on outward mechanics. We need books penned from hearts that are fully engaged and invested in a lifestyle of prayer.

We need growing revelation in the value of intercessory worship that is both corporate and continual. This is God's weapon of choice to change the spiritual atmosphere of the cities of the earth. Do not approach this book as just another book on prayer. God wants to change your paradigms and priorities. Make an altar with God, and receive a holy resolve to enter into an abandoned lifestyle called "Unrelenting Prayer."

Mike Bickle
Director, International House Of Prayer of Kansas City
www.IHOP.org

Then He spoke a parable to them, that men always ought to pray and not lose heart, saying: "There was in a certain city a judge who did not fear God nor regard man. Now there was a widow in that city; and she came to him, saying, 'Get justice for me from my adversary.' And he would not for a while; but afterward he said within himself, 'Though I do not fear God nor regard man, yet because this widow troubles me I will avenge her, lest by her continual coming she weary me.'" Then the Lord said, "Hear what the unjust judge said. And shall God not avenge His own elect who cry out day and night to Him, though He bears long with them? I tell you that He will avenge them speedily. Nevertheless, when the Son of Man comes, will He really find faith on the earth?"

(Luke 18:1-8, NKJV)

1

NEVER RELENT!

"Nevertheless, when the Son of Man comes, will He really find faith on the earth?" (Luke 18:8).

Have you been seeking God a long time for your break-through? Then know this: The devil wants you to give up!

He'd like to convince you that God has ignored your prayer or is refusing to act on your behalf. "Face it," your enemy croons, "nothing is going to change."

But you? You've got your fingers wrapped around Promise.[1] Your jaw is set, your gaze is fixed, and you'll never stop contending for the release of Kingdom power and authority in this generation. And because of your tenacity, you now find yourself in the battle of a lifetime. Why?

---

[1] "Promise" (singular) will be capitalized in this book because the Holy Spirit is called "the Promise" (Acts 1:4). Promise is a Person. When you have hold of Promise, you have hold of a piece of God.

Because your prayer life has stirred up a spiritual hornet's nest. You've become a dangerous endtime weapon in the hand of your God, and your adversary is enraged.

The greatest warfare always surrounds your prayer life. Nothing threatens hell more than the praying saint. When you're abiding in His presence, clinging to His love, living in His Word, holding to His Promise, remaining fervent in spirit, and believing for His visitation, you're an explosion that's waiting to happen. Don't think your enemy will let you inhabit God's promises unchallenged.

When you stand at the throne of God and lift your unrelenting cry to your Judge, always asking and seeking and knocking, you won't have to go looking for a fight—it will find you. Because your enemy knows if you will just stand there—and never be silent and never lose heart and never give up, but lift your voice to your Judge until He gets justice for you—eventually something is going to happen. It's inevitable. You are standing on the platform that rewrites human history. Most assuredly, God is going to rise up on your behalf and answer your cry. And the certainty of God's intervention makes you dangerous to the enemy's agenda. So he will come against your resolve to pray and will do everything in his power to move you from before the throne. *Anything to get you to shut up!*

WILL HE FIND FAITH?

The battle to pray *and to keep on praying* has never been fiercer. Predicting that the intensity of this warfare would increase as His return draws near, Jesus asked a piercing question, "'Nevertheless, when the Son of Man comes, will He really find faith on the earth?'" (Luke 18:8).

What did Jesus mean by His question? In His primary

meaning, Jesus was asking a question about His second coming to earth. "When I return to the earth at the end of the age—at the time when the saints will be severely tested by Satan's rage and by a worldsystem that will abandon itself to darkness—will I find My people living in such a reality of faith that they will be crying out to Me incessantly in pure confidence and expectation? Or will Satan's scheme to snuff out My people's faith be successful?" By posing the question, Jesus was indicating that faith is not an automatic shoo-in. The question should haunt our hearts as a dreadful warning. Will the forces unleashed against the saints in these last days be so formidable that we lose the kind of authentic faith that prays through to fulfillment?

Jesus' question also has a secondary and more immediate meaning. In His question, we can hear Him implying, "When I come to visit you personally and to answer the cry you first uttered long ago, will I find you still looking to Me and calling upon Me in full assurance of faith? Or will I come to answer your prayer only to discover that you've lost heart, given up hope, and fallen back into silent resignation?"

The Lord rarely tells us in advance when He will come to us with the answer. He said, "'Watch therefore, for you do not know what hour your Lord is coming'" (Matthew 24:42). If He were to tell us when our prayers would be answered, we would not know how to steward that kind of information wisely. It could break us, ruin us, wound us, discourage us, or disorient us. Under ongoing pressure we naturally inquire, "How long, Lord?" Our hearts search, like those of the prophets,[2] to discover the manner of time in

---

[2] According to 1 Peter 1:10-11, the prophets searched the Spirit of God carefully to try to see both the what and the when of God's coming salvation.

which God intends to fulfill His plan. But often our understanding of timing is blurred. Faith postures itself, therefore, to be ready and alert at all times, always prepared through unceasing prayer for the visitation of God. *Jesus, when You come to visit us, may You find us watching!*

AN EMPOWERING PARABLE

The words from Luke 18:8 quoted at the top of this chapter were spoken in the context of a powerful parable—a parable which is the fountainhead of this book. In relaying the parable to us, Luke precedes Jesus' words with his own helpful commentary:

> *Then He spoke a parable to them, that men always ought to pray and not lose heart (Luke 18:1).*

Prayer is to be incessant and unrelenting until the answer comes.

We need not construe or conjecture what Jesus meant in giving us the parable of Luke 18:1-8 because Luke states Jesus' meaning from the outset. Christ strategically designed the parable, Luke explains, to empower the prayer lives of His people. Jesus wants us to pray always and believe for the fulfillment of Promise. *Prayer is to be incessant and unrelenting until the answer comes.*

The greatest temptation when waiting for God's answer to your prayer is to lose heart. To become faint-hearted. To be discouraged to the point of despair. To give up hope. To conclude you don't have what it takes, in this instance, to move heaven on your behalf. To decide that nothing is going to change.

Delayed answers by nature tend to cause us to lose

heart. "Hope deferred makes the heart sick" (Proverbs 13:12). This heartsickness is a natural human response when we are waiting on God for a long time. But then the enemy comes to add his demonic fuel to the fire. He interjects his doubts and lies, doing everything in his power to cause us to lose heart. The challenge to remain in faith in the face of God's delays can seem almost overwhelming at times.

Make no mistake about it, there is a mocking spirit that has been launched from hell as part of Satan's end-time strategy to pummel God's people into faintheartedness. Peter warned us that this voice "will come in the last days...saying, 'Where is the promise of His coming? For since the fathers fell asleep, all things continue as they were from the beginning of creation'" (2 Peter 3:3-4).[3] In other words, the mocking voice says, "Nothing has changed. So where is the Promise of God's intervention? Nothing has changed because *nothing is going to change*. You're waiting for something that's never going to happen."

There isn't a praying saint who, clinging to God's promises, hasn't heard that sneering, taunting voice of unbelief. That's why Jesus gave this parable. It is brilliantly designed to empower us to persevere in confident prayer until the answer is released.

The closer Christ's return, the more difficult it is to contend for the supernatural. The enemy wants you to believe that since you live in such an empirical, rationalistic,

---

[3] A similar skepticism is articulated in Isaiah 5:19, where men say of the Lord, "'Let Him make speed and hasten His work, that we may see it; and let the counsel of the Holy One of Israel draw near and come, that we may know it.'" The psalmist expressed his pain over dealing with this mocking spirit, "As with a breaking of my bones, my enemies reproach me, while they say to me all day long, 'Where is your God?'" (Psalm 42:10).

post-modern, digital age, you cannot expect divine inter-vention. "Miracles may have been experienced in more primitive times," says the logic from below, "but with all our technological advances and modern conveniences, how can we expect God to intervene for us who have so much?" Some Christians, buying into the enemy's drivel, have stopped contending for healings, miracles, sovereign provision, deliv-erance, and heart-arresting encounters with the supernatural power of God.

To have faith, by definition, is to pray and keep on pray-ing and never lose heart in prayer.

That's why this parable is more relevant and crucial today than ever. Because of the warfare we face, we desperately need the faith this parable imparts.

PURSUING FAITH

Let's return to the quote with which we started this chapter.

"Nevertheless, when the Son of Man comes, will He really find faith on the earth?" (Luke 18:8).

This parable, you see, is about faith; it's all about faith. To have faith, by definition, is to pray and keep on pray-ing and never lose heart in prayer. Persevering prayer is in itself an expression of faith. The only reason you per-sist is because you believe. Faith always prays; unbelief stops praying. If you had stopped bringing your requests to God or thanking Him for the answer, that would have been evidence that unbelief had taken over your heart. Unbelief says, "My life is slipping away from me; I've got to do something different." But faith says, "I'd rather die than stop contending for Promise." Faith prays until the answer comes.

O how our hearts long to touch mountain-moving faith! Peter described this quality of faith as "precious" (2 Peter 1:1) and "much more valuable than gold" (1 Peter 1:7) because it endures for eternity. Every advance in faith is taken with us to the next age. This caliber of faith is one of the greatest and most challenging pursuits of the devout life. If it were so easy to obtain, more people would have it. Understanding the difficulty of attaining mountain-moving faith, Paul urged us twice in his writings to "pursue faith" (1 Timothy 6:11; 2 Timothy 2:22). The climb is arduous, but the glory of the goal makes it a most noble pursuit deserving of our best energies.

Rees Howells had an expression, "The meaning of prayer is answer."[4] He held the conviction that prayer which didn't procure its answer was meaningless. If ever a generation needed the kind of faith that procures answers to prayer, it's ours! How our hearts long for the sublime glory of what Charles Price called "meeting our Savior in the garden of answered prayer."[5]

The thing we most long for—answered prayer—is the very thing the adversary is most resisting in this final hour. We're in the battle of the ages. When Jesus asked whether He would find faith on the earth at His coming, He was forewarning us that faith will be greatly contested in the last days. May the alarming timbre of Jesus' question cause us to throw off the cords of lethargy, rise up in a holy indignation, and answer from the depths of our being, "Y-e-e-e-s! We will be men and women of faith! We will

---

[4] Norman Grubb, *Rees Howells, Intercessor;* CLC Publications, Fort Washington, PA, 2001, p. 41.

[5] Charles S. Price, *The Real Faith For Healing,* North Brunswick, NJ: Bridge-Logos Publishers, 1997, p. 4.

not forfeit our place of prayer and fall into temptation. We will never stop pleading the promises. We will call upon heaven without ceasing because we believe the promises of God. We know that You are determined to invade our world with Your limitless power. So we will cooperate with You in intercession until it happens."

Beloved, there is a day when Jesus *will* come to us. And when He comes, He will look to see whether we are still contending for resurrection power with unabated tenacity and confidence. If He finds us calling on His name in genuine faith, He *will* render justice for us against our adversary. We *shall* see the power of God in our generation! Therefore we will never relent.

2

GOD LOVES JUSTICE

Then He spoke a parable to them, that men always ought to pray and not lose heart, saying: "There was in a certain city a judge who did not fear God nor regard man" (Luke 18:1-2).

Let's begin by becoming acquainted with the characters of our parable. Jesus starts by introducing us to a very evil man, an unjust city judge.

This judge had no fear of God. In other words, he had no concern for the fact that one day he would stand before God Almighty to give account for the rectitude of the judgments he passed. He felt accountable to no one, not even God. Therefore, he was susceptible to all kinds of vice such as greed, corruption, extortion, intimidation, favoritism, and the like.

King David wrote, "The Rock of Israel spoke to me: 'He who rules over men must be just, ruling in the fear of

God'"(2 Samuel 23:3). But the judge of our parable shared nothing of David's conviction.

Furthermore, he had no regard for man. In other words, he had no pity for the plight into which men sometimes fall. Mercy or compassion? Not from this man. When he saw violation or abuse, there rose within him no righteous indignation to defend the neglected or victimized.

An evil man such as this would serve as judge for but one reason: personal advantage. He cared only for his own enrichment, so quite often the person with the largest bribe would win the case. This man dispensed judicial decisions based upon bribery and personal favors. There was no justice to be found at his bench.

When you cannot find justice at the seat of justice—the courts of the land—where do you turn? As the Scripture says, "If the foundations are destroyed, what can the righteous do?" (Psalm 11:3). When justice does not reside at the seat of judgment, the land inevitably falls into social anarchy. Thus, Jesus was describing a land ruled by lawlessness.

COMPARISON AND CONTRAST

Our parable contains both similarity and contrast. In terms of his office, this judge is *similar* to God who is "'the Judge of all the earth'" (Genesis 18:25). Like God, the judge is the ultimate authority within his jurisdiction. Whatever sentence he passes is immediately enforced. There is no further appeal. But that's pretty much where the similarities end.

For the most part, Jesus intends for us to view this evil, unjust judge in *contrast* to God. This human judge had no regard for man; but your Heavenly Father, in stark contrast, takes keen, personal interest in every human being. He sees every way in which you have been wronged, and He longs to bring healing and closure where you've been violated and abused. Your heavenly Father loves you with an everlasting love (Jeremiah 31:3), so when you come to Him with your complaint, you are coming to One who embraces you and welcomes the opportunity to grant you a hearing.

Furthermore, quite unlike the evil judge, God *loves* justice! If there's anything important to God, it's justice—that it be recognized, honored, implemented, and maintained. To uphold justice is one of God's core values, one of His most fundamental convictions. This is why Jesus called justice one of the weightiest matters of the Mosaic law.[1]

GOD'S ZEAL FOR JUSTICE

One of the things that angers God most is when He sees men perverting or neglecting justice. Many of His commands were warnings against this kind of violation. Furthermore, it's especially important to God that justice be given to the widow or orphan.

> *"You shall not afflict any widow or fatherless child. If you afflict them in any way, and they cry at all to Me, I will surely hear their cry; and My wrath will become hot, and I will kill you with the sword; your wives shall be widows, and your children fatherless" (Exodus 22:22-24).*

---

[1] "'Woe to you, scribes and Pharisees, hypocrites! For you pay tithe of mint and anise and cummin, and have neglected the weightier matters of the law: justice and mercy and faith'" (Matthew 23:23).

The reason this passage is important to this book is because the parable of Luke 18 involves a widow (we'll come to her in Chapter 3). The unjust judge is going to be approached by a widow, and he is going to try to deny her justice.

When you cry to God for justice, He responds not only because He loves you, but also because He loves justice.

God has deep-running feelings about this. He purposely went on record as being passionately committed to providing justice for widows. The unjust judge is going to be unmoved by the fact that the person coming to him is a widow. God wants it clearly understood that He is nothing like this unjust judge. *He is totally committed to getting justice for the grief-stricken.*

God sternly said to the people, """"Execute judgment in the morning; and deliver him who is plundered out of the hand of the oppressor, lest My fury go forth like fire and burn so that no one can quench it, because of the evil of your doings'""" (Jeremiah 21:12). God is severely against those who have it in their power to deliver the oppressed but do not do so—because He Himself would never fail to do so. God is basically saying, "When there is injustice, and I have it in My power to execute justice, I am zealous to do so. And I expect the same of you."

Beloved, when your adversary rises up against you, you can be assured of this truth: Your God loves justice, and He is *zealous* to avenge you of your adversary! Here is a sampling of verses that reveal God's zeal to execute justice:

- God is a just judge (Psalm 7:11).
- The King's strength also loves justice (Psalm 99:4).

- He loves righteousness and justice (Psalm 33:5).
- For the LORD loves justice (Psalm 37:28).

That's why the Scripture says, "It is a joy for the just to do justice" (Proverbs 21:15). The Just One, our God, finds it the joy of His heart to avenge us. He couldn't have said it more clearly: "'For I, the LORD, love justice'" (Isaiah 61:8). When you cry to God for justice, He responds not only because He loves *you*, but also because He loves *justice*.

In this respect, our Father is the exact antithesis of the unjust judge in this parable. Now that we've met the unjust judge, let's go to the next chapter to look at the other two characters in our parable—the widow and her adversary.

3

THE IRREPRESSIBLE CRY
FOR JUSTICE

Now there was a widow in that city; and she came
to him, saying, "Get justice for me from my adver-
sary" (Luke 18:3).

It is striking that Jesus couches this parable in the imag-
ery of a widow. When we envision a widow, we might
think of someone who is weak, lonely, poor, defenseless,
and lacking societal influence. However, the most compelling quality about a widow is *bereavement.* There has
been a death in the family—specifically, the death of her
husband.

Some of you can relate to bereavement in a very personal way because you too have had a death in your family—literally. For others, death has come to your household
in a different way. You may have experienced the death of
a marriage, or the death of a cherished relationship, or the
death of lifelong dreams and aspirations, or the death of

financial equilibrium, or the death of a career, or the death of mental or emotional health, or the death of physical well-being and vitality, or some other form of death.

Bereavement is one of the most common human experiences. When we think of bereavement, we immediately associate it with emotions such as sorrow, heartache, feeling out of control, heaviness, grief, despondency, and mourning. Thus, the widow in the story represents a host of emotions that most of us have experienced or will experience in our lifetimes. When we broaden the definition of bereavement to include the loss of something very precious, instantly most of us can identify with the widow's feelings and emotions.

THE ADVERSARY

Little is said in the parable of the widow's adversary. Whoever he (or she) was, he probably saw this widow as an easy target. If he could successfully devour her, he could have her house and possessions. Her adversary was willing to use whatever diabolical means were necessary to exploit her vulnerability, destroy her, and confiscate everything she owned.

Beloved child of God, I hope you are fully aware of this reality: *You have an adversary.* His name is Satan. Together with his demons, he is bent on ripping you off and bringing you down. His only agenda for your life is to steal, to kill, and to destroy (John 10:10). The warfare is not mystical and ethereal; it's tangible and real. You are engaged in the most epic of all battles, against an enemy who hates you with a perfect hatred.

Well, it's not so much that he hates *you* but that he hates *God*. He can't get to God directly, however, so he does the next best thing. He assaults God by attacking you.

The prophet wrote to God's people, "'He who touches you touches the apple of His eye'" (Zechariah 2:8). The apple of the eye is another term for the pupil of the eye. The pupil is the most sensitive member of the entire body. We blink involuntarily in the face of danger because the body's first instinctive reflex is to protect the eye. When you get a speck in your eye, the whole universe stops until you get it out. By calling us the pupil of His eye, God was saying He is as protective over us as we are over our eyes. Satan knows that when he strikes us, God takes it in the eye. So he connives ways to inflict maximum damage upon our lives in order to strike at God.

I am not impressed with Satan's ability to attack us, but rather with God's ability to protect and keep us. As I once heard Jack Taylor put it, "Big God, little devil." However, the wise believer is not flippant about the sober nature of the spiritual warfare which surrounds us. Our adversary will wait for a moment when we're feeling secure and our guard is relaxed, and then he'll hit us in ways we least anticipate. There are no holds barred in this fight. No means of attack are too dastardly or beneath his dignity to employ. No shot is too cheap. We live in a war zone, and the wise will maintain constant vigilance regarding the wiles of the devil.

Satan knows that when he strikes us, God takes it in the eye.

Sometimes we may find ourselves in a war zone, taking hits from an unseen enemy, and we don't know how to respond because we don't understand the nature of the warfare. When this happened to me, I was alarmed because I lacked discernment regarding the nature of what was coming against me. I didn't know where my enemy was, so I didn't know how to protect myself. But the Lord comforted me with David's prayer in Psalm 69:19, "My adversaries are all before You." David meant, "Even when I don't know who my enemies are, Lord, nor the nature of what is coming against me, You do." I may not know the source of the warfare, but I know the One who does. He sees my enemies. He knows every strategy against me, and He is able to deliver me from every evil thing and present me to Himself without fault and with great glory. In this is all my hope and trust.

THE JUDGE'S AUTHORITY

The adversary was targeting the widow, and the only possible defense she had was the evil judge in her city. Although she knew he was evil, she had nowhere else to turn. He was the only one who had authority to dispense justice for her, so to him she came.

You will notice that she didn't go to her adversary for justice. If she had gone to her adversary and said, "I am asking you to stop this and to treat me right," her adversary would have laughed in her face. She was weak and poor, and he was strong and powerful. She had no power over her adversary, so she went to the one who had jurisdiction over him. She went to the judge.

Our models of spiritual warfare may need some adjustment in this regard. In going after the devil, some of us have tried to wring justice from him by saying things like, "Satan, we command you to restore what you've stolen, in Jesus' name!" And then we wonder why nothing changes. Was that a snicker we just now heard?

Satan's not about to get me justice! If I tried to appeal to him, he would just sneer at me. He won't relinquish even an inch of ground unless he's strong-armed into it.

No, I'm not going to talk to my adversary; I'm going straight to my Judge. I may not be able to match Satan's strength, but he is no match for the God I serve! So I will bring my complaint to my Judge, who has authority over my adversary, and I will cry to Him until He extracts justice for me from my adversary.

TAKING A STAND

Suffering the malevolence of her adversary, the widow decided to place herself before the judge and cry out to him until he acted on her behalf.

I can imagine this widow saying in her heart, "When God lifted His hand against me and snuffed out my husband's life, I suffered in silence. And then, when people drew their own conclusions and made judgments about me—yes, I knew they were talking about me and imagining what I might have done to incur such punishment—I suffered the reproach of people in silence. But now an adversary has risen up against me, and *I will be silent no longer!* I may not have any social clout, and I may not have any money to pay off the judge, but this much I have: I have a cry. So I will lift my voice and cry to my judge until I get justice from my adversary!"

By lifting her voice to her judge, the widow was exemplifying spiritual warfare. As the enemy engaged her, she engaged the judge. We respond the same way to attacks from the powers of darkness. Paul spoke clearly about our struggle with demonic powers (Ephesians 6:11-18). He made it clear that spiritual warfare involves putting on the whole armor of God and then withstanding and standing firmly. "And having done all, to stand"

(Ephesians 6:13). But our warfare is not limited to stand-ing, nor does it stop there. Once our stance is firm and we have put on the full armor of God, then comes the next phase of our warfare: "praying always with all prayer and supplication in the Spirit" (Ephesians 6:18). In other words, crying out to God. The purpose of the believer's armor is to protect and empower him or her for prayer. We stand so that we can pray. That's what the widow was doing. She was standing and crying out to her judge, which models for us the nature of true spiritual warfare. You don't just stand; you stand and pray.

And the form of prayer we use? Paul called it "all prayer." When we pray with "all prayer," we invoke any and every possible expression of prayer available to us, such as thanks-giving, supplication, intercession, singing, rejoicing, weep-ing, calling, pounding, worship, adoration, commanding, waiting, entreaty, dancing, laughing, travail, rest, presenting requests, etc. We put on the armor of God so that we might stand and cry out to our Judge, using the full spectrum of prayer's expressions, until He acts on our behalf.

When we emulate our widow, take our stand before our heavenly Judge and cry out to Him for justice from our adversary, the battle takes on a new twist. The adversary, seeing us standing and calling upon the Lord, becomes alarmed and changes his tactics. He begins to target our resolve to stand before God.

The enemy knows that if you will just stand there, and never be silent, and never be moved, but lift your voice to your Redeemer until He gets justice for you, eventually something is going to happen. God will inevitably step into action and supernatural power will be released. Di-vine promises will be fulfilled, and you will be equipped with a testimony that will empower the next generation.

In other words, a major setback for Satan.

That's why every device of darkness against your life is focused upon one single issue: To move you from standing before God.

We do not wrestle with principalities and powers in order to wrest from them the justice we desire. We're wrestling over standing rights. They're trying to get us to compromise our stand and to shut our mouths. But we will not give up our stand before the throne of God nor will we be silent! We will resist every device of darkness to move us. Nothing will stop us from lifting our cry to our Judge.

> *Every device of darkness against your life is focused upon one single issue: To move you from standing before God.*

THE DESIGN TO MOVE YOU

It all comes down to standing and crying. Will you stand and cry, or can you be dissuaded? As long as you're standing before God and continuing in prayer, nothing can stop your spiritual destiny. But if you can be moved from the place of prayer—from the place of gazing upon the face of Christ—then everything God has planned for your life is at risk.

Hell expends its best ammunition on trying to move you from before the throne. The enemy has three primary strategies for accomplishing this. He will try to *distract* you from the place of unrelenting prayer; or he will try to *tempt* you away from God's presence; or he will seek to *discourage* you from standing before God.

Distraction. Temptation. Discouragement. Those three words summarize the struggle of every single reader. All three will eventually visit us in the seasons of life, but at any given moment our struggle will typically be strongest in one of those three areas. So one of the three is probably your "biggy" right now. Which is it for you? Do you find yourself easily distracted from your place before God— through the cares of life, the busyness of business, the demands of the calendar? Or does the enemy target you with temptation to compromise your moral standards? Or does he seek to overwhelm your soul with discouragement, despair, and aimlessness?

I've known all three, and you probably have too. Because all three will eventually take turns with us. The design of darkness is to do anything to move you from the most powerful posture that a human can employ. *Anything—to get you to shut up! Anything—to get you to lose heart! Anything—to move you from your platform before God.*

The widow had to endure all of her adversary's abuse, and not allow it to stop her from crying out to the judge. Distraction and temptation and discouragement must have wracked her soul, but we aren't told about that aspect of her struggle. To gain practical insight into that kind of fight, therefore, we'll need to look elsewhere. Someone who fought—and conquered—these devices of darkness was Joseph.

Like the widow, Joseph was a friend of sorrow and grief. He was also on a journey toward greatness. The enemy saw Joseph's trajectory toward spiritual greatness and tried everything in his power to dissuade Joseph. Let's look at how Joseph overcame these three schemes of darkness.

HOW JOSEPH OVERCAME

Joseph was determined to stand before God. Even

when he was torn from his family, hauled to Egypt, and sold into slavery, he still lived in communion with His God. The enemy wasn't about to let Joseph hold that high ground without contesting it, however, so he launched his assault by trying to *distract* Joseph from God's presence. This was done simply by giving Joseph a promotion. Joseph was promoted to being steward over his master's entire holdings. It became his responsibility to oversee every aspect of a very diverse household and business. He was tempted to neglect the presence of God, and it could have seemed so justifiable—"Lord, You're the One who gave me this job," I can imagine him musing, "and You know how many hours I have to work in order to be faithful to my employer. Surely You must be pleased with how diligent and responsible I am in the job You've assigned me." Joseph could have used this kind of logic to justify neglecting the presence of God. But no, he refused to allow the demands of his obligations to rob him of the one thing he held most precious. Above all, he had to know the gentle movements of God upon his heart. So he jealously guarded his relationship with God.

When distraction didn't work against Joseph, the enemy pulled scheme number two from his arsenal—*temptation*. This is where Potiphar's wife came in (Potiphar was Joseph's master). Potiphar's wife tried to seduce Joseph repeatedly, day after day, but he kept denying her overtures. Finally, she grabbed hold of him and tried to pull him into bed, but he slipped out of his cloak, left it in her hands, and ran outside. Enraged at being spurned, she concocted a story that incited her husband to throw Joseph into prison. But the point is: Joseph passed the temptation test. He would not let temptation cheat him of his intimacy with God.

I've often wondered, "How did Joseph do it? How did he muster the inner resources to run from the temptation?" After all, I reckon Potiphar's wife was no dog, and Joseph was a very normal young man. Yet he said, "No." I think the answer lies in Joseph's awareness of the spiritual inheritance that awaited him. He knew God had promised great things to his fathers, Abraham, Isaac, and Jacob; and he discerned that he was next in line to receive the blessing. But he also realized that moral compromise could disqualify him from God's highest and best. Joseph understood he could not burn with God's fire and also burn with her fire. He had to decide which fire he wanted burning in his soul. To have God's fire, he would have to reject her fire.

Joseph understood he could not burn with God's fire and also burn with her fire.

He looked at his spiritual inheritance, saw the fiery exhilaration that God had destined for his life, and chose to burn with God's flame rather than temptation's flame. He passed the test!

But the enemy wasn't finished with Joseph. He still had his best card to play. If Joseph was to be moved from before God's throne, nothing could strike him with greater impact than this last great device of darkness—*discouragement.* What would be the vehicle for this discouragement? Imprisonment! When Joseph was thrown into prison, discouragement tried to overwhelm his soul and drown out the flame of his heart. Beyond all question, Joseph struggled intensely with discouragement in prison. However, he refused to let it push him out of the presence of God. Even in his depressing circumstances, he remained a man of prayer who lived in the presence of God.

Joseph conquered all three of Satan's greatest devices: distraction, temptation, and discouragement. And because of it, he rose to the highest place of privilege in the nation of Egypt. He became a world leader who served the nations of the earth and also provided for his own people, the children of Israel. Truly he was "more than a conqueror."

Joseph's tenacity to stand before God and cry for deliverance was just like that of the widow in Jesus' parable. She was determined to stand before her judge and cry to him, regardless of what her adversary would throw at her.

JESUS' TEMPTATION

How can we stand resolutely before the throne of God when our adversary is assailing us? There is no greater example of an overcomer than that of our Master Himself. When accosted by the adversary, Jesus had to fight to maintain His stand. In the wilderness temptation (see Matthew 4:1-11), Satan did his utmost to move Jesus from the place of prayer.

The devil launched his attack by saying, "If You will just bend over and pick up a stone and turn it to bread…"

Jesus said, "I'm not bending over. I'm going to stand right here."

So the devil said, "If you will just throw Yourself down from the pinnacle of the temple in a sensational way…"

Jesus said, "I'm not throwing Myself down; I'm just going to stand here."

So the devil said, "Well, if you will bow down and worship me, then I'll give You everything…"

"You don't get it," I can hear Jesus responding. "I'm not going to bend down, I'm not going to throw myself down, and I'm not going to bow down. I'm going to stand—and having done all, to stand!"

Our widow responded to her adversary in the same way. She would not be moved from the place of crying out to her judge. So we're going to adopt the same posture before God! We will come to His throne, stand in His presence, and lift our voices to Him until He gets justice for us from our adversary.

A JUST CLAIM

When the widow presented her case to the judge, she knew she had a valid grievance and that the law was on her side. If only she could get justice, then her adversary would be properly judged. To use Isaiah's term, she had a "just claim." In other words, she had a legal basis for her request. Here's where Isaiah coined the phrase a "just claim":

> *Why do you say, O Jacob, and speak, O Israel:"My way is hidden from the LORD, and my just claim is passed over by my God"? (Isaiah 40:27).*

We also have many "just claims" before God. A just claim is any legal right we have to God's provision. When God makes a Promise to His family, and we're part of that covenant family, then we have a legal right to stand and claim that Promise for ourselves. When we present our just claim to God, we are not being arrogant or presumptuous. We are simply asking for that which is rightly ours as covenant children.

It's important, when coming before the Judge, that you have a just claim. If He takes up your case and then discovers you don't have a just claim to what you're asking, you could end up in more trouble than when you started.[1] Be sure, therefore, that your request is according to the will of God.

But when you have a just claim, you can come to your Father with confidence and know that He loves to execute justice where your enemy has stolen, killed, and destroyed.

We may tend to think of justice in a very narrow way, such as punishment for a crime. But justice is a far-reaching term, as wide in its scope as every conceivable form of evil. Even as injustice afflicts men and women in virtually every arena of life, justice is the righteous answer to every wrong.

When justice comes to sickness, there is healing.
When justice comes to poverty, there is provision.
When justice comes to infirmity, there is wholeness.
When justice comes to loss, there is restoration.
When justice comes to torn relationships, there is
    reconciliation.
When justice comes to anarchy, there is order.
When justice comes to imprisonment, there is
    release.
When justice comes to reproach, there is
    vindication.
When justice comes to rejection, there is acceptance.
When justice comes to abuse, there is comfort.
When justice comes to prejudice, there is equity.
When justice comes to oppression, there is liberty.

---

[1] An example of that is found in Acts 18:17, where Sosthenes took a beating at the judgment seat of Gallio because he brought a complaint to the judge that was not a just claim.

When justice comes to slavery, there is freedom.
*When justice comes to tyranny, there is
    compassionate leadership.*
When justice comes to crime, there is punishment.
When justice comes to wrong, there is right.
*When justice comes to indebtedness, there is
    repayment.*
*When justice comes to death, there is resurrection
    life.*
*When justice comes to destruction, there is
    reparation.*
When justice comes to calamity, there is relief.
When justice comes to hunger, there is nourishment.
When justice comes to weariness, there is rest.
When justice comes to fear, there is peace.
When justice comes to violation, there is dignity.
*When justice comes to barrenness, there is
    fruitfulness.*
*When justice comes to abortion, there is protection
    for the unborn.*
When justice comes to darkness, there is light.
When justice comes to pain, there is alleviation.
When justice comes to blindness, there is sight.
When justice comes to families, there is unity.
When justice comes to dysfunction, there is health.
*When justice comes to loneliness, there is
    companionship.*
When justice comes to depression, there is joy.
When justice comes to anxiety, there is confidence.

O Lord, receive my just claim, and get justice for me from
my adversary!

4

HARASSED TO ACTION

"Now there was a widow in that city; and she came to him, saying, 'Get justice for me from my adversary.' And he would not for a while; but afterward he said within himself, 'Though I do not fear God nor regard man, yet because this widow troubles me I will avenge her, lest by her continual coming she weary me'" (Luke 18:3-5).

The judge stalled in taking on the widow's case because he knew she had no bribe in her hand. He had nothing to gain by taking on her case, and he thought he had nothing to lose by brushing her off. So he put it on the shelf and hoped she'd go away.

But this little lady wasn't about to go anywhere. After all, where else could she turn? Her only hope was to somehow persuade the judge to take up her case. How could she persuade him, though? She could think of only one approach: Badger the man until he relents.

I can imagine the widow finding creative ways to harass the judge. She can't hassle him on his own turf, but the moment he walks out of his office, there she is. "Get justice for me from my adversary!"

He swings by the food market on his way home, and suddenly there she is in the olive oil aisle. "Get justice for me from my adversary!" The judge can hardly step onto public property without being accosted by this persistent widow. He says to her, "Yackety-yak, lady, give it a rest! Do you ever shut up?" She retorts, "No. Not ever."

He takes his wife out for a romantic dinner. They're enjoying a delicious meal by candlelight, and everything about the evening is perfect. They step out of the restaurant and BOOM, there she is. "Get justice for me from my adversary!"

His wife says, "You better do something about that woman, or you won't have a marriage." This selfish judge is painted into a corner. He doesn't want to hassle with the widow's case, but he realizes it's either that or be hassled for the rest of his life.

A literal rendering of the original wording in verse 5 would read like this, "Lest unto the end coming she harass me." In other words, the judge realized this woman was going to keep coming after him, if need be, right up to the very end—even unto death. If he would not get justice for her, the only thing that would silence her would be the grave. And although this man was wicked, even he was unwilling to use murder as the means of dispensing with her.

So, to preserve his sanity and personal comfort levels, this judge finally concluded he had no option but to rise up and execute justice on her behalf. She pestered him until he caved in.

GOD AND THE JUDGE CONTRASTED

There is one parallel between God and the judge in this portion of the parable. Just as the judge stalled to get her justice, in a similar way, God sometimes also delays to provide justice for us. His reasons for doing so, however, are altogether different from the unjust judge's, which we will see shortly.

In every other respect, God and the judge are to be viewed as opposites. For example, the widow and the judge were at each other's necks; but our relationship with our heavenly Father is the exact opposite. It's a totally tender relationship. Unlike the widow, we have an *affectionate partnership* with our Judge. We partner with Him, through intercession, to implement justice in the earth. Unrelenting prayer is the vehicle by which we enter into partnership with Christ. As a lovesick Bride, we invest our tears and cries into the cause; then, when the breakthrough comes, we're exhilarated with exceeding joy because we've had ownership of the process.

We partner with our Judge, through intercession, to implement justice in the earth.

Here's another contrast between God and the judge: The judge executed justice for selfish reasons, but God gets justice for us for totally different reasons. God is motivated, not by self-interest, but by selfless love. Nor does He make decisions based upon His own comfort levels—a truth that is emblazoned powerfully in the cross of Christ. The cross demonstrates God's willingness to pay the penultimate price tag—the life of His only begotten Son—for our sakes.

Furthermore, God is not hassled nor inconvenienced by us. When we plant our feet at His throne and determine to call on His name without respite, He is not wearied by our importunity but rather is moved by it. He *loves* it! He welcomes our heartsick cries.

He says, "I love it when you set your eyes on Me alone and decide that I am your only Savior and Deliverer. I love it when you call upon Me and never lose heart, but continually offer prayers to Me with thanksgiving. I love it when you decide to wait on Me until you see My glorious salvation. I love to see your face, hear your voice,[1] and behold your heart as it is fixed steadfastly upon Me. This is all that I've ever wanted from you!"

GOD LOVES UNCEASING PRAYER

It's fascinating but true: God *loves it* when we cry out to Him, day and night, without ceasing. Why? Because He reckons unrelenting prayer to be an expression of faith. He sees it as a concrete representation of the confidence we have in His intervention. And if there's anything that pleases God, it's faith (see Hebrews 11:6).

If you had no faith, you would have given up asking by now. The fact that you're still asking is, in itself, evidence of a measure of faith, even if you wish your faith levels were stronger. Unceasing prayer is by essence a declaration of confidence in God's will and intention to intervene. So when you lift your cry 24/7, God receives your demonstration of faith with great pleasure and delight.

This is why He exhorts us to ask and keep on asking, to seek and keep on seeking, and to knock and keep on knocking.[2] When we read the command, "Pray without

---

[1] See Song of Solomon 2:14.

[2] This is the literal meaning of Matthew 7:7.

ceasing" (1 Thessalonians 5:17),[3] we must see it as coming from the heart of a Father whose heart yearns for communion with us.

David, a man after God's own heart, was also a man who strove to pray without ceasing. His heart was so sincere about this that, on one occasion, he said to the Lord, "Let my prayer be set before You as incense" (Psalm 141:2). Incense has this property of lingering in the air long after the smoking embers have been extinguished. David was saying, "Lord, let my prayer arise in Your presence as a continual reminder—even during those moments when I am physically unable to engage in prayer. Even when I'm sleeping, may the fragrant incense of my prayers continue to stand before you as a witness to the great cry of my heart."

The Lord totally delights in this Davidic passion to live in a place of constant prayer. We bring Him pleasure when we resolve in our hearts to make prayer a 24/7/365 reality in our lives. The evil judge was inconvenienced by the widow's cries, but God is the total opposite. He couldn't have said it more clearly: "The prayer of the upright is His delight" (Proverbs 15:8).

THE WIDOW AND THE ELECT CONTRASTED

God and the judge are not the only ones contrasted in this parable. There are also compelling contrasts drawn between the widow and God's elect. We identify with the widow in the way she experienced bereavement and loss, and in the way she cried out without ceasing; but there is one crucial aspect in which we must see ourselves in

---

[3] We find a similar command in Ephesians 6:18, "Praying always with all prayer and supplication in the Spirit."

stark contrast to the widow.

And it's this: The widow is bereaved of a caring husband; the elect of God, on the other hand, are described in the Bible as an espoused fiancée. We are the Bride of Christ, engaged to our Lord as a chaste virgin (see 2 Corinthians 11:2). Far from having lost our Husband, He is alive and well, and we have a most glorious inheritance in Him!

So we do not come to our Judge as a forlorn widow who has no husband; we come as the Bride of Christ, carrying the authority that He affectionately confers upon His betrothed. We know that we are "the yearning of His heart,"[4] so we have absolute boldness in approaching the Judge's bench.

We come before Him with unapologetic confidence. We have been brought into His family, born of incorruptible seed,[5] and now we enjoy the relational leverage of impressing our inner longings upon the One who loves us so intensely.

He who did not spare His own Son, but delivered Him up for us all, how shall He not with Him also freely give us all things? (Romans 8:32).

Your Beloved cannot turn away from you for you have won His favor and ravished His heart. Now He will move heaven and earth, if necessary, to provide for His dearly beloved Bride. *You are His elect, and He loves you!*

The Scriptures reveal times when God intervenes supernaturally on our behalf because of this love relationship that has been developed between us. Here

---

[4] See Isaiah 63:15.
[5] 1 Peter 1:23.

are three of the more compelling instances in Scripture that witness to this reality:

> *He delivered me because He delighted in me (Psalm 18:19).*

> *"Because he has set his love upon Me, therefore I will deliver him" (Psalm 91:14).*

> *"Eye has not seen, nor ear heard, nor have entered into the heart of man the things which God has prepared for those who love Him" (1 Corinthians 2:9).*

There are many things God does for us simply because He loves us so much.

WHEN INTIMACY ISN'T ENOUGH

However, the Lord has also revealed that an intimate love relationship is not always the only element necessary to unlock every Kingdom door. To open some doors requires intimacy plus a second ingredient. The necessity of this second ingredient is confirmed clearly in the parable Jesus gave us in Luke 11:5-8 (which is actually a parallel parable to our primary text). Here's the parable of Luke 11 to which I'm referring:

> *And He said to them, "Which of you shall have a friend, and go to him at midnight and say to him, 'Friend, lend me three loaves; for a friend of mine has come to me on his journey, and I have nothing to set before him'; and he will*

answer from within and say, 'Do not trouble me;
the door is now shut, and my children are with
me in bed; I cannot rise and give to you'? I say
to you, though he will not rise and give to him
because he is his friend, yet because of his per-
sistence he will rise and give him as many as he
needs. So I say to you, ask, and it will be given to
you; seek, and you will find; knock, and it will be
opened to you" (Luke 11:5-9)

In this parable Jesus uttered these startling words,
"though he will not rise and give to him because he is
his friend." Jesus was showing that, while friendship is a
powerful force, the strength of friendship is not always
enough to motivate a friend to act on behalf of his friend.
Sometimes there are mitigating circumstances.

Jesus was basically saying, "Friendship with God alone
will not always produce answered prayer. Sometimes
there are other extenuating circumstances which require
more than just intimacy to move the hand of God."

In recent years, the Holy Spirit has been emphasizing
the centrality of intimacy and friendship with Jesus in believers' lives. Consequently, many today are discovering
deeper levels of communion with Jesus. He has been gently assuring us, "You are not a widow; you are My Bride."
Because of the Spirit's emphasis of this reality, many of us
are gaining confidence in our bridal identity before Jesus.
We have a growing understanding of how attractive and
desirable we are to Him.

And yet, despite a growing confidence in love, many
continue to have the evidence of answered prayer still
unfulfilled. The temptation, in that hour, is to question the
legitimacy of our intimacy with Christ and the validity of

our friendship with God. We find ourselves wondering, "If I really have the closeness with Jesus that I think I have, why does He spurn my cry? If I delight His heart, why does He not deliver me?" It can be tempting to wrongly conclude that He is not as ravished over our fervency and devotion as we had thought.

Or it can be tempting to become offended at God, get angry, and say things like, "Lord, I'm Your friend, and yet you're blowing me off. What kind of a Friend are You anyways? You have the power to deliver me, and yet You look upon the pain of Your beloved and continue to stonewall me. Some kind of friendship we must have!"

When these kinds of accusations want to grip our souls, the parable of Luke 11 is a necessary reminder, for it provides unique insight into the heart of God. It reveals that, when God does not immediately answer our prayer, we should not automatically conclude that there is something wrong in our relationship. Jesus' perspective is essentially the same as the man in the house who said to his friend, "There's more at work here than just our friendship. There are issues of timing and other elements complicating the situation. Our friendship is still good; it's just that it's not the only factor I'm working with."

The dimension of answered prayer portrayed in Luke 11:8 was based upon two elements. It was based, first, upon friendship. The strength of their friendship had given the man the confidence to approach his friend for the bread he needed. Without the friendship he would have never mustered the boldness to ask at such a late hour. However, Jesus clearly reveals that *friendship alone is not always a strong enough basis for producing answered prayer.* Friendship is a factor, but it's not the only factor. So what is this second ingredient that must be added to intimacy? In a word, it's *persistence*—persistence in knocking and asking.

Jesus was clearly teaching that *persistence receives what intimacy alone does not.* Why is this so? Because God views persistence as a substantial[6] expression of faith, and it is faith (together with love[7]) that pleases God[8] and triggers supernatural intervention.[9]

When you're tottering emotionally, wondering why your intimacy with God doesn't seem to be effect-

Persistence receives what intimacy alone does not.

ing any change, the enemy will usually come to add his accusations to the pile: "You're deceived. You think you've got this great thing going with God. But look, He won't even answer your prayer. The intimacy you think you have with God is all a farce."

Jesus uses the principle of Luke 11:8 to whisper His truth to your heart: "You need never question My love for you. You are My Bride and you ravish My heart! But there's more going on here than just our friendship. Your enemy wants you to get offended and give up. That is the totality of his agenda. Don't go there. Keep loving! Keep asking! Keep seeking! Keep contending! The key to your breakthrough will be found through unrelenting prayer. Persist in the prayer of faith, and you will gain the answer."

So our widow did it right, after all. She kept after the judge until he avenged her. This is the model of prayer that Jesus wants branded into our souls. He wants us to pray without ceasing, with a tenacity that is not put off even when nothing seems to be changing. It is this kind of persistence that stirs God to action.

---

[6] See Hebrews 11:1.
[7] 2 Timothy 1:13; Galatians 5:6.
[8] Hebrews 11:5-6.
[9] Matthew 17:20; 21:21.

5

DAY AND NIGHT
INTERCESSION

Then the Lord said, "Hear what the unjust judge said. And shall God not avenge His own elect who cry out day and night to Him, though He bears long with them?" (Luke 18:6-7).

Now Jesus changes gears and makes the parable applicable to His hearers. He does so by posing a rhetorical question, "If an unjust judge will grant justice to an unrelenting widow, shall not your righteous God avenge His own chosen ones who cry out to Him day and night?" The answer is self-evident: "Yes! God *will* avenge His own elect who call on His name."

Beloved, you are the elect of God. As His eyes went to and fro over the face of the earth, He stopped when He saw you and said, "This one. I want *this* one." You have been hand-selected by God. He had many other options, but He wanted *you*.

"Elect" means "chosen ones." As the chosen of God, you are His favored one—the object of His desires and dreams—the longing of His heart. His affections run so strong and deep for you that words fail to describe the vast dimensions of this love. Given His profound affection for you and given your unremitting faith, there can be no mistaking the outcome. God *will* answer your prayer.

THE POWER OF DAY AND NIGHT PRAYER

Prayer in itself is powerful. But it's even more powerful when it becomes incessant. Notice that Jesus said the elect "cry out day and night." Sure enough, the Holy Spirit is igniting day and night intercession in this final hour, and it's for no small reason. Here are but a few of the benefits of unremitting prayer.

IT SEALS FIERY AFFECTIONS

In the last days, one of the greatest designs of darkness is to cause our love to grow cold (Matthew 24:12). The best way to maintain a fiery spirit in love is through prayer. When we stop praying, we cool off. So how can we be sure to remain steadfastly fervent? By praying always (Luke 21:36; Ephesians 6:18).

In these last days, the intensity of spiritual warfare is increasing. The devices of the devil that are designed to make us wartime casualties are becoming more sophisticated and accessible to us. The only thing that will keep us effective in the Spirit, burning in love, and vigilant in warfare is nonstop prayer (see Ephesians 6:18).

Unceasing prayer is the great secret that ushers us into an abiding relationship with Christ. There is nothing more powerful in the spirit realm than the saint who has learned to abide in the love of Christ. When we are joined to Him in intimacy and affection, it is inevitable that we will become much more fruitful in the Kingdom. While we're still waiting for justice, the intimacy cultivated through unrelenting prayer makes us fruitful even during the wait. One reason the wait can be so long is because the Lord is totally retraining our living patterns, so that when the breakthrough comes we don't return to old patterns. Breakthrough without intimacy is deadly. When God finally avenges us, it will be more important than ever to be established in the fiery intimacy that was gained during the wait.

Even though the breakthrough may still be withheld, unrelenting prayer has the surprising effect of actually increasing our passion for Jesus. Analyzing the thing logically, we might expect God's delays to make us bitter and cause us to shut down toward Him; but in actuality, His delays have the opposite effect. In desperation, we draw near to Him and cry out to Him with unprecedented fervency. We press into His Word like never before. And in the process of that passionate pursuit, He awakens us to His beauty, glory, grace, and profound affections for us. The harder we come after Him, the more lovesick we become!

If we had prayed a quick prayer and gotten a quick deliverance, we may have never pressed with such intensity into the Word and the Spirit. But because we persevered in prayer, now we are ablaze with passionate delight in the glory of the Man, Christ Jesus.

IT EMPOWERS HOLY LIFESTYLES

The apostle Paul wrote, "Therefore, as the elect of God,

holy and beloved" (Colossians 3:12). Paul pointed to two qualities of the elect:"holy and beloved."The elect of God are His beloved, His loved ones, and the objects of His fiery affections. But the elect are not only beloved, they are also holy. When the elect cry out to God day and night, they are choosing to stand in the holy place 24 hours a day. They are taking up a lifestyle of holiness. It's impossible to pray 24/7 without holiness. So the fact that the elect are praying 24/7 is a reflection of their commitment to holiness. There is nothing more powerful before God than the mixture of "beloved" and "holy." If you were only "beloved," that alone would activate God's intervention on your behalf. But add "holy" to the mix, and now you're unstoppable! Holy and beloved—nothing can defeat that.

IT SUSTAINS AND NURTURES FAITH

Unrelenting prayer procures answers, but it does more than that. It also empowers the saint to remain in faith during the wait. When we stop praying, our faith immediately flags and diminishes. Word-based prayer has the power of keeping us in faith, even when God bears long with us. That's why Jesus prayed on the cross. He never stopped praying during His crucifixion for He knew it was unrelenting prayer that would keep Him from losing heart and would empower Him to persevere all the way to resurrection. Jesus may have had lengthy periods of silence on the cross, but even though vocally silent, He never ceased praying.

I've sometimes wondered if Jesus Himself may have also prayed our prayer while on the cross, "Get justice for Me from My adversary." If He did in fact offer that prayer, there is no uncertainty about the outcome—the Father most certainly avenged Him of His adversary![1]

If it was prayer that enabled Jesus to remain in faith during the entirety of His sufferings, how much more must we pray always so that we might not lose heart in the journey!

IT REAPS A HARVEST

Real believers always pray without growing weary, for they are totally convinced of the principle of Galatians 6:9—"And let us not grow weary while doing good, for in due season we shall reap if we do not lose heart." The principle in this verse is simple: If you sow to the Spirit, you will eventually reap of the Spirit. Believers keep sowing steadfastly in prayer, for they know they will eventually reap a harvest if they do not lose heart. Sow tears in your season of sorrow and one day you will reap a harvest of joy (Psalm 126:5)!

IT KEEPS US SPIRITUALLY ATTENTIVE

Unrelenting prayer is designed, by nature, to keep us alert and spiritually proactive during the waiting season. Hebrews 6:12 makes it clear that we cannot become sluggish in the journey and expect to inherit promises. Promises are inherited by those who maintain their fervency and spiritual diligence regardless of the length of the journey. The example cited in Hebrews 6:13 is that of Abraham. Abraham would not allow himself to become spiritually sluggish, even though he ended up waiting

---

[1] Actually, Jesus has been avenged of His adversary only in part. The full vengeance yet awaits, to be manifest in the final Day of the Lord.

25 years for the Promise to be fulfilled. The heart of the Abraham-like saint says, "I don't care if I have to wait 50 years! I will never relent but will offer myself in unceasing prayer, activating my spirit and abiding in Promise, until I am avenged of my adversary."

IT POSITIONS US FOR OBEDIENCE

Prayer keeps us in a posture of listening, and listening is essential to obedience. It's when we hear that we're able to obey (James 1:25).

This principle is illustrated graphically in the life of a man named Ananias. Saul of Tarsus was apprehended of God, blinded by a heavenly light, addressed by an audible voice, and sent to Damascus for further instructions. Now that God had Saul in Damascus, he needed a servant to send to Saul with heaven's instructions.

The problem was, all the believers in Damascus had heard that Saul was coming to town to arrest all the Christians. Many of the believers already had fled town. Others were cowering in fear in their hiding places. God was looking for someone who was abiding constantly in prayer, but the ranks had suddenly evaporated.

I can imagine an angel bringing a good report. "Lord, we've finally found someone who is unrelenting in prayer. There's still one man standing. We've never heard of him before—his name is Ananias—but he is standing firm in prayer and has not left his post."

"Good," I can suppose God saying, "He's Our man. Send Ananias to Saul with my message." Ananias received the assignment to commission Saul (whose name was later changed to Paul) to his apostolic ministry. This honor was given to Ananias because he was unrelenting in prayer.

In heaven right now, Ananias is famous for being the guy who commissioned Paul to his ministry. Imagine another believer meeting Ananias in heaven for the first time.

"Hey, aren't you the guy who prayed for Paul to receive his sight?"

"Yes."

"Well, tell me about it."

"Actually," I can hear Ananias countering, "That's not the only thing I did. That was only one tiny moment in my ministry. I actually had a whole lifetime of ministry before the Lord. Wouldn't you like to hear some of my other stories?"

"Sure. But maybe another time. For right now, I'd just like to hear about the time you prophesied Paul into his ministry."

My point is, that after a lifetime of labors, Ananias is famous in eternity for one solitary act of service. If he had not been praying and listening on that day, he would have missed the greatest opportunity of his life.

Would you be willing to give yourself to a lifetime of unrelenting prayer if it meant being available for one single moment of obedience?

Ananias had one shot at greatness. The issue was whether he would be in prayer when that instant arrived. Because he was found standing steadfastly in prayer at the crucial moment, he was ready to obey when the call came.

Pray without ceasing, beloved! A lifestyle of prayer makes you available to God 24/7. Who knows, perhaps God will tap you at the moment you least expect, and will call you to one act of obedience that will forever change your destiny and empower your testimony on the day of judgment. Will you be found standing in prayer when your opportunity for greatness comes?

IT PRESERVES US IN THE BREAKTHROUGH

God will use a lifestyle of day and night prayer, during the waiting season, to establish us in intimacy. These new depths of intimacy and love are absolutely essential for what's coming, so that when the Lord finally brings us through to deliverance, the temptations that come with multiplied open doors don't damage us. One of the greatest temptations, when the answer comes, is to neglect intimacy, become self-determining and independent, and lose our way in the midst of God's blessings.

After the breakthrough, people will pull on us; they will want to hear our testimony; the demands on our life will multiply. Intimacy is our safeguard. God will sometimes wait with His deliverance until we have established through 24/7 prayer a lifestyle of intimacy that will not unravel under the strain of the next season of fruitfulness. It's the lovesickness that God is producing within us during the wait that ends up protecting us when the answer comes.

God loves us too much to allow the blessing to break us. So He uses the delay, strategically, to immerse us in intimacy so that, when the answer comes, we won't lose our way.

In light of the many benefits of 24/7 prayer, it should come as no surprise that the Holy Spirit is igniting day and night prayer in our generation in an unprecedented manner.

THE NECESSITY OF DAY AND NIGHT PRAYER

According to our parable, Jesus said the elect cry out to God "day and night." Thus, Jesus was endorsing day and night prayer. More than endorsing it, He was urging it. But even more than urging it, He was prophetically announcing its certainty. "In the last days," Jesus was predicting, "my people *will* be found crying out to God day and night."

Why is day and night prayer at the top of God's agenda today? Because it's in the context of day and night prayer that speedy justice will be released to God's people. We pant for the endtime release of God's Spirit, but it will come only in concert with unrelenting prayer. The present movement in the body of Christ toward 24/7 worship and intercession is not accidental or incidental. It is the response of the Bride to a strategic press of the Holy Spirit in this final hour as He prepares the earth for Christ's return. The Lord wants His people calling upon Him day and night, and night and day, and day and night, and night and day. As the elect accept the Spirit's invitation to day and night prayer, the purposes of God are accelerated in the earth, and we move so much more quickly toward the consummation of the ages. This is one crucial way we cooperate with God in "hastening" Christ's return to earth (see 2 Peter 3:12). Through 24/7 prayer, we place a demand upon heaven that literally brings the Kingdom of heaven to earth.

90-minute Christianity will not answer the intensity of today's battle.

Join the 24/7 prayer movement! Get in on the action! 90-minute Christianity[2] will not answer the intensity of today's battle. No, the Holy Spirit's agenda in this final hour will require incessant vigilance and the constant invoking of any and every kind of prayer. Lift your cry and never relent! Cry out for speedy justice.

---

[2] I am referring to the modern practice of limiting one's involvement in Christianity to 90 minutes once a week on Sunday mornings.

Cry out in the day—when you have light for your path and are enjoying the sun of God's blessings. The temptation, in the time of warmth and light, is to relax, kick back into an enjoyment mode, and become sporadic in prayer. Never allow the brightness of your day to diminish the intensity of your cry.

Cry out in the night—when you are living in darkness and have no light for your path. The times of darkness produce a desperation of heart that can kindle your fervency in prayer, but as the night season grows long, you can become tempted to lose heart and revert to a survival mode. Don't allow the prolonged darkness of your night to silence your cry. Cry out—day and night!

Our parable describes a polarization that will characterize the church at the end of the age. Because of the pressures that are coming upon the saints in these days, they will have one of two responses: to either lose heart and give up praying, or to devote themselves to unabated, intense, 24/7 prayer. The pressures of the hour will cause the in-between categories to vaporize. It will become all or nothing. May we be among those who go 24/7!

When Jesus closed the parable with the question, "'Nevertheless, when the Son of Man comes, will He really find faith on the earth?'" (Luke 18:8), He was indicating that this parable has particular relevance for the final generation in which the Lord returns. In those final days—days in which we are most certainly living—one of the characteristics of that age will be protracted seasons of crying out for justice, with God bearing long with His elect. Do not be shaken by the wait, nor consider that this is something strange that is happening to you.[3] The wait is an important part of God's

---

[3] 1 Peter 4:12.

training process in your soul, and you will overcome only through unrelenting prayer.

For thousands of years the saints have cried out to their Judge, "Get justice for us from our adversary!" And God has borne long with us. But the speedily of God is coming. Matthew 24:34 makes clear that the last days' events will unfold and be consummated within the span of a single generation, which means there will be a dynamic acceleration of divine activity at the end of the age. The speedily of God is coming to our entire planet! Therefore, 24/7 prayer is more crucial today than ever.

THE NATURE OF DAY AND NIGHT PRAYER

For prayer to be sustained day and night, it must have a certain quality about it. This quality is found in Psalm 77.

In the day of my trouble I sought the Lord; my hand was stretched out in the night without ceasing; my soul refused to be comforted (Psalm 77:2).

The psalmist speaks of seeking the Lord in the day, and then reaching out to the Lord in the night without ceasing. He is describing 24/7 prayer. And here's what he has to say about that kind of intense seeking: "My soul refused to be comforted." In other words, "I am calling upon God with every atom of my being and with all my strength. Therefore, I am not going to settle for second best or some kind of consolation prize. I'm not interested in a stopgap measure that temporarily props up my soul but delivers nothing that produces a testimony. I'm not

My soul refuses to be comforted!

simply looking for relief or for a way to cope with life's disappointments. I'm contending for the demonstration of the mighty salvation of my God!"

Unrelenting prayer is never satisfied with anything less than fullness. However, when you stake your claim and lift your cry to your Judge, your adversary will try to talk you into accepting something less. He doesn't want you entering into the fullness of your inheritance in Christ, so he'll try to convince you that you're going to have to settle for some paltry, measly alternative.

This kind of talk holds no water with those who are committed to praying day and night until they see breakthrough. If you're willing to pay the price of 24/7 prayer, you're certainly not going to accept some cheap consolation prize. No, your soul refuses to be comforted with anything less than total justice from the throne of God.

Moses was a man who refused to be comforted with anything less than the fullness of God's salvation. But even so, Pharaoh did his best to try to talk Moses out of fullness. Three times he tried to convince Moses to accept something less than complete deliverance. Here was Pharaoh's first attempt.

> *Then Pharaoh called for Moses and Aaron, and said, "Go, sacrifice to your God in the land"* *(Exodus 8:25).*

Moses had told Pharaoh that they must make a three-day trip into the wilderness in order to sacrifice to the Lord, but here Pharaoh was saying, "I'll let you go, as long as you stay within the borders of Egypt." But Moses declined Pharaoh's offer. He refused to be comforted with a plan that wouldn't allow them to exit Egypt.

Then Pharaoh tried this one on Moses:

So Moses and Aaron were brought again to Pharaoh, and he said to them, "Go, serve the LORD your God. Who are the ones that are going?" And Moses said, "We will go with our young and our old; with our sons and our daughters, with our flocks and our herds we will go, for we must hold a feast to the LORD." Then he said to them, "The LORD had better be with you when I let you and your little ones go! Beware, for evil is ahead of you. Not so! Go now, you who are men, and serve the LORD, for that is what you desired." And they were driven out from Pharaoh's presence (Exodus 10:8-11).

As a concession, Pharaoh was offering to release them to hold their feast to the Lord if just the adults would go and the children would stay behind. Pharaoh knew that if the children remained in Egypt, the adults would most certainly return. But Moses refused to be comforted by this offer, either. He wasn't about to lose the next generation to idolatry. No, the children must come and worship together with the adults. Moses would be satisfied with nothing less than the entire family.

Pharaoh made one final attempt at conciliation.

Then Pharaoh called to Moses and said, "Go, serve the LORD; only let your flocks and your herds be kept back. Let your little ones also go with you" (Exodus 10:24).

In this compromise, Pharaoh was saying, "Okay, you can take your children with you. Just leave all your flocks and herds back here in Egypt." But Moses refused to be comforted with this one, either. He knew they would need their flocks and herds so they could offer to the Lord their God the proper sacrifices that would be fitting once they came out of Egypt. Three times Pharaoh tried to talk Moses into accepting a compromise, but Moses refused to be comforted with anything less than total deliverance.

Our enemy still tries to use these kinds of arguments with us today. "Just stay here in the land of bondage. Worship God, but accept the fact that this place of imprisonment is to be your home forever."

"You can worship God with all your heart and soul, just don't expect to take your kids with you. Since you're married to an unsaved spouse, you can't expect your kids to serve God. And your divorce—it left an indelible mark on your kids; they're ruined for life. And that nasty experience you had in your former church? Your kids have never recovered from all that spiritual abuse, nor will they. Face it, you've lost your kids. Serve God for yourself, but your kids are mine."

"Worship God with your family, but don't let your faith leak over into your career. Your livelihood and profession is not the place for your faith. Keep that separate, and just worship God within the confines of your four walls."

These kinds of offers ring in the ears of God's saints all the time, especially to those who are holding out for the manifestation of God's promises in their lives. But like Moses, we won't be comforted until we have received everything for which we are contending. Because Moses refused to be comforted with anything less, he got it all. The sacrifice happened outside the land of bondage, with all the women and children, and with all the flocks and herds. Like the Israelites in Moses' day, we refuse to settle for anything less than the fullness of God's salvation!

When you're holding out for God's highest and best, you view the pain you're in as an incentive to pursue God harder. You're not interested in simply dulling the pain, lest your pursuit of God also be dulled at the same time. So you're not comforted by a prescription, a drug, food, drink, entertainment, recreation, a caffeine pick-me-up, or illicit sexual release. You refuse to be comforted by anything but the full-blown manifestation of the resurrection life of Christ!

Allow me to be personal for a little bit. As of this writing, I have been waiting on God for 13 years for His promised healing of an affliction in my voice. I continue to pound heaven's doors with unrelenting prayer. The temptation to settle for a consolation prize has come to me personally in a variety of ways, but I am refusing to be comforted. Some people will say to me things like, "Well, really, when you look at your life, it's really not that bad. Compared to other people, you could be a whole lot worse off." The inference is, "If you don't receive the answer to your prayers, you're still not that bad off." To that line of reasoning I have one thing to say: *My soul refuses to be comforted.* I will not settle for coping with the adversary's plunderings simply because others have experienced worse devastation than I.

Some of my friends have said, "Well, Bob, even if the Lord never heals your voice, look at how your voice is going forth in the earth through your writings. You have more of a voice now, without a voice, than when you had your voice. Furthermore, consider how he's changed your heart in this season, deepened your understanding through revelation, and brought you into a sweetness of intimacy with Jesus. Even if you're never healed, surely it has been worth it!" I have just one response to such reasoning: *My soul refuses to be comforted.* I am thankful to God for His preservation in my life—I'm amazed that I'm still here and still in the battle; and I'm so grateful for the favor He has showered upon both me and my family. But I refuse to be satisfied merely with preservation and favor. I want justice from my adversary! And I will not desist from 24/7 prayer until He gets justice for me from my adversary.

Others of my friends have asked me, "Bob, have you explored some of the latest advances in medical technology? There are innovative surgical procedures available today that weren't available even ten years ago." I appreciate their sincerity, but *My soul refuses to be comforted* with a measure of relief that some new kind of surgery might afford. I've come too far in this journey through darkness to settle for that. No, my soul will be satisfied with nothing less than God's justice.

Others have asked me, "Have you considered suing the doctor who did this to you?" (I had a bad surgical procedure in 1992 that damaged my vocal apparatus.) One brother in Christ wrote me a very sincere letter once, urging me strongly to consider suing the doctor. He said I wouldn't be suing the doctor personally, I would be suing his insurer. He told me that doctors pay malpractice insurance premiums specifically for the benefit of people like myself who have suffered from a surgical error. He said he recognized that I was not angry or bitter over my experience, but that I should sue simply as a means of getting the kind of financial settlement that is rightly due someone who has suffered a blow to their professional career because of a doctor's mistake. His letter was gentle and kind with no vindictive element in it. But when I read it I thought, "I'm going to sue, all right. But not in any court on earth. I'm suing in heaven." I'm not interested in getting a merc million dollars, and then crawling into a cave somewhere and finding ways to cope with my lot for the rest of my life. No, *my soul refuses to be comforted* with that. I want a far greater settlement than a lousy million bucks! I want heaven to get me justice from my adversary. I want the devil to rue the day he came against this servant of God. I'm contending for restoration and restitution.

Another question I get frequently is, "Have you thought about learning sign language?" Many who ask that question will follow it up with something like, "Deaf people would certainly benefit from receiving your message if you could sign to them." When people make those kinds of comments to me, I nod and smile politely. But inside I'm thinking, *"My soul refuses to be comforted with that!"* You see, beloved, I haven't come through this living hell, battling demons, wrestling with principalities, enduring storm and darkness, merely to learn how to sign to the deaf. No, I'm contending for something far more valuable—I'm fighting for the power and authority in the Spirit to open the ears of the deaf and release them from their prison of physical infirmity. I understand what it's like to be incarcerated by a physical handicap, and once you've done time in that prison, the greatest passion of your heart becomes to see the prisoners set free. My soul will be satisfied with nothing less than the release of the Luke 4:18 anointing that rested upon our Lord Jesus and has been promised to us today. My heart is steadfast; I will not relent from 24/7 prayer until I see the manifestation of "so great salvation" in my day and generation.

Day and night prayer is the kind of prayer that refuses to be comforted with partial blessings. Like our widow, we will not relent until we get total justice from our adversary.

6

THE CONTROVERSY

"And shall God not avenge His own elect who cry out day and night to Him, though He bears long with them?" (Luke 18:7).

And now we come to the controversial part of the parable—"'though He bears long with them.'"To understand the controversy surrounding this phrase, we must first understand the actual, literal wording of the text. *Berry's Interlinear Greek-English New Testament* shows a word-for-word rendering of the original text:

> *"And God not shall execute the avenging of his elect who cry to him day and night, and [is] being patient over them?"*[1]

---

[1] Berry, George Ricker, *Berry's Interlinear Greek-English New Testament*, Grand Rapids, MI: Guardian Press, 1976, p. 213.

Such a word-for-word rendering makes for awkward reading in the English. The verse reads more smoothly and is equally accurate in the Darby Translation:

> *"And shall not God at all avenge his elect, who cry to him day and night, and he bears long as to them?"*

The most literal rendering of the last part of the verse would be, "and being long-tempered over them?" Most translators, however, avoid the expression "long-tempered" because it is clumsy in the English language. The American Standard Version comes closest to this:

> *"And shall not God avenge his elect, that cry to him day and night, and yet he is longsuffering over them?"*

The translations just mentioned, together with other scholarly translations such as Weymouth's, J.B. Phillips', Webster's, and Wesley's, all render the verse in a way that is accurate to Jesus' intent. However, most of the English translations that are currently popular make a grave error in translating this verse. Herein is the controversy.

The reason many modern translators have grappled to know how to render the verse is because there is a powerful paradox in the parable—one which we will examine shortly. They saw the seeming contradiction and didn't know what to do with it. So instead of just translating the verse as Jesus spoke it, they decided to adjust Jesus' words in such a way as to eliminate what they saw as a contradiction. They thought they were doing us a service by eliminating the paradox, but in fact they have done us a disservice by putting into Jesus' mouth words that He did not utter.

When we "help Jesus out" by telling others, "Well, Jesus didn't mean it exactly the way it appears at face value—what He *really* meant to say was such-and-such," we are walking a treacherous path. I call it treacherous because we are in danger of being rebuked by God Himself. I myself have been directly rebuked by God for thinking I could improve on Jesus' words, so I know first-hand how treacherous this ground can be. When the Holy Spirit rebuked me for my arrogance and error, I quickly awakened to the realization that Jesus had the brainpower to say it exactly the way He meant it. So I did some fast repenting. I no longer rework the words of Jesus; I now let His words rework me.

Back to our translators. Many of them have made the unfortunate error of moving beyond the scope of *translation* and stepping onto the ground of *interpretation*. When a work claims to be a *translation* but then steps from the boundaries of a translator's work over into interpretation, we find ourselves on shaky ground. In contrast, when a composition claims to be a *paraphrase*, there's room for interpretation because the reader understands that the editors are not attempting an accurate translation of the original languages, but are injecting their own creative interpretations and linguistic embellishments into the text. When we know up front that we're reading a rendering with interpretive flair, then we don't mind so much when an author misses the precise meaning of the original text. For example, the popular paraphrase "The Message" misses it on Luke 18:7, but we don't mind so much because it's a paraphrase. What is problematic is when we *think* we're reading a translation but then do not get the actual meaning and intent of the original text.

Get ready, I'm about to do some translation-bashing. The reason I'm about to lambaste how some of today's most popular Bible translations render Luke 18:7 is because they don't merely miss the meaning of Jesus' words, they actually have Him saying *the exact opposite* of what He said. And the implications are *huge*.

So if you use the New International Version, your translation is coming under fire. If you prefer the New American Standard or the Revised Standard Version, then your translation is also going to take a hit. Same for the Amplified Bible. All these popular Bibles make the same dread mistake in translating Luke 18:7. They take the last phrase of the verse and turn it into a second question.

For example, the RSV renders it, "'And will not God vindicate his elect, who cry to him day and night? Will he delay long over them?'" By turning the last phrase of the verse into a second rhetorical question, the answer to the second question would most naturally be, "No. God will not delay long over them." But that's not what Jesus is saying or inferring at all. In fact, He's saying the opposite.

The translations mentioned above are not the only English[2] translations to make this mistake; I only mention them because they are among the most widely used. Most translations—in English as well as other languages—make the same mistake, however. They have Jesus telling us, in so many words, that God will not delay long over His beloved elect.

---

[2] Incidentally, English translations are not the only ones to misrepresent the actual wording of Luke 18:7. Every other language I've checked to date makes the same mistake, such as the German, Russian, and Spanish Bibles.

When they have Jesus saying that God will not delay to bring justice to His elect, they set God's people up for a lot of perplexity and duress. Believers, then, don't know what to make of those times when God does, in fact, bear long with them. It sets God's people up to draw all kinds of wrong conclusions both about God and themselves. "Is God mad at me?" "Is there unresolved sin in my life?" "Does God not fulfill His promises?"

The NIV, RSV, NASB, and Amplified Bible are wrong. They tell us that God does not delay to answer our prayers, but it's simply not true. Jesus does not pose two rhetorical questions in verse 7. Rather, He asks one rhetorical question, followed by a qualifying phrase. If you have the King James Version you win—the KJV gets it right. Or if you have the translation used in this book—the New King James Version—you win.

The NKJV renders it accurately: "'And shall God not avenge His own elect who cry out day and night to Him, though He bears long with them?'" Jesus was not suggesting that God would not delay long over His people; to the contrary, He was saying that God sometimes *does* bear long with His elect. *Sometimes God listens to the cries of His people for a long time before acting.*

Anyone who has been with the Lord for a period of time knows there is no question about it. Sometimes God waits a long time to answer our prayers.

Jesus was saying, "God shall most certainly avenge His elect who cry to Him day and night. And even if He bears a long time with them and withholds His answer for a seemingly long period of time, there is no question about the certainty of the outcome. Before the story is finished, He will avenge His loved ones."

MORE CONTROVERSY

But it's not the translators alone who have a controversy with the verse. The theologians have a controversy
over it as well. The controversy surrounds this weighty
question: "When it's God's will to answer a prayer, does
He always answer it right away, or does He sometimes
wait with the answer, even when the prayer is offered in
fullness of faith?" The issues surrounding that question are
gigantic and have spawned all kinds of theological camps
and positions.

There are two theological extremes to this question,
and neither extreme is accurate. I'm going to take the liberty of poking in a light way at both extremes. I think I'm
safe in parodying the two ends of the spectrum because
there are relatively few people who would throw themselves fully into either extreme. Hopefully we can all smile
together at these excessive positions and, in the process,
grow in understanding.

There is one school of thought in the body of Christ
that says, "Lift your cry to your Judge. Cry out for justice.
And if you cry the right cry, in the right way, you will get
justice *immediately* from your Judge."

You like the idea of an instantaneous breakthrough,
so you decide to do it their way. You lift your cry to your
Judge and then start looking for an immediate change. If
nothing happens immediately, the folks in this "now camp"
will come alongside and help you tweak your cry. "Here,
try crying it like *this*," they say. So you adjust your cry and
lift your voice again to heaven. If there is still no immediate result they will come to coach you again, "Okay now,
cry to God *this way.*" So once again you tweak your cry.

Folks in this camp will work with you for a little while.

But there soon comes a point where, if you haven't received your answer, they will decide you're a hopeless case and will be finished with you. They may say things like, "You're a double-minded man, unstable in all your ways, and you shouldn't think you'll ever receive anything from God." They adopt this position because they lack a theological framework for a God who waits to perform His will.

There's another school of thought in the body of Christ that is on the other side of the issue. These folks will say to you, "Lift your cry to your Judge. Cry out for justice. Present your best case before the throne. But after you have offered your deepest cry, then you need to leave your petition with God and surrender the outcome to His sovereignty. Because His ways are not our ways, and His thoughts are not our thoughts. Since God is so much higher than us, you can never be 100% certain that you know the perfect will of God in regard to your request. So the best you can do is offer your cry, relinquish it all to God, and learn to cope with whatever comes down the pike."

This camp has lots of theological space for God to take His time. In fact, it's okay with them if you're not healed until after you die and go to heaven. They'll say at your funeral, "Now she's healed." This is how they comfort you. "God will answer your prayer," they assure you, "either here or in the next life." They think this teaching is the most compassionate way to encourage people whose fate appears hopeless.

The fact is neither camp represents the truth. The true teaching of Scripture, from Genesis to Revelation, is summarized succinctly and powerfully by the Master Himself—in Luke 18:7. The truth is: It *is* the will of God to avenge His elect who cry to Him for justice; however, sometimes He will strategically wait a long time before rising up in judgment.

Occasionally the two positions enter into combat, and you can watch the war on Sunday morning TV all across America. Channel 4 is saying you have the right to an immediate miracle, while Channel 6 is telling you to accept how God, in His wisdom and providence, chooses to answer your prayer.

Just this past weekend I was ministering in Maryland and turned on my hotel TV on Sunday morning to listen to some preaching while I was getting dressed. A popular program was being broadcast, and they said in so many words, "You don't have to go one more day without your miracle. We will teach you how to have faith, and if you will pray with us and believe, you will receive your answer immediately." For those who receive an immediate miracle, this message is tremendously positive and faith-building. But for those who don't see an immediate answer, the opposite tends to happen. Concluding they don't have enough faith to move heaven on their behalf, they become gripped with heartsickness. In other words, they lose heart and stop asking. And that's the *last* thing Jesus wants them to do! He is saying, "Do *not* lose heart! Keep crying out to your Judge. He may be bearing long with you, but be assured, if you keep crying out to Him day and night, He will most certainly avenge you!"

Jesus was clearly saying that prayers of faith are not always answered immediately.

With one little phrase ("though He bears long with them"), Jesus divulged an immensely important insight into the ways of the Father. He tipped us off to the fact that sometimes the Father does not answer our prayers immediately, even though they are offered in faith and affection. Jesus was clearly saying that prayers of faith are not always answered immediately. That truth comes directly and irrefutably from the Master's lips in Luke 18:7.

That's why this parable is so critically important in this hour. It corrects those who say, "Just wait until heaven," and it corrects those who say, "Faith receives immediately, every time." But the parable does more than present accurate theology. Better than that, it *empowers* believers with faith and endurance to run their race until they gain the prize. Without this parable, the temptation to lose heart could be overpowering. With this parable, we are equipped to remain constant in prayer and expectation, thus becoming a formidable force that partners with Christ to bring the Kingdom to earth.

WHY THE WAIT?

The verse says God bears "long" with His elect, so I did a word study on the original Greek word for "long." I discovered its true meaning. The word means "long."

But why does God sometimes wait so l-o-o-o-o-o-ng?

I remember hearing the Spirit's gentle whisper, "Wait on Me." I was not so encouraged when I received that word. I was thinking, "Lord, You're in a different time zone. With You, a day is as a thousand years. By the time You get around to acting on my behalf, I may be six feet under ground."

I began to wonder, what is it with God and the waiting thing? Why does He like it so much? So I asked the Lord, "Of all the tools at Your workbench, why do You always reach for that one? 'Wait on Me. Wait on Me.' It seems to be the only answer I ever hear. Don't You have any other tools at Your disposal? Why is the waiting thing Your favorite?"

It's a crucial question with an important answer. When God bears long with His beloved elect, it is because He has strategic purpose in the wait. And He doesn't want us ignorant of His purposes.

If we are to pray 24/7 and not lose heart while God bears long with us, it is absolutely essential that we gain living understanding into purpose. We must be convinced that God has *redemptive purpose* in waiting to avenge us, and that His judgment will *most certainly* come to us at just the right time—with the suddenness and impact of a freight train. When we know this we will not lose heart. More than that, the day will come when we will actually thank God for the delay. Why? Because we are seeing His redemptive purpose in it.

So…why does God wait?[3] Here are a few reasons He bears long.

GOD WANTS TO SHOW HIS WRATH AND GLORY

When we wait in faith for God to avenge us, the wait gives God the legal leverage before Satan to do much more for us than if we had received immediate relief. This principle is reinforced in the book of Romans:

> *What if God, wanting to show His wrath and to make His power known, endured with much longsuffering the vessels of wrath pre-pared for destruction, and that He might make known the riches of His glory on the vessels*

---

[3] To explore this question even further, I commend my earlier book, *The Fire Of Delayed Answers,* which delves into this question much more in-depth than the book you're now holding.

of mercy, which He had prepared beforehand for glory, even us whom He called, not of the Jews only, but also of the Gentiles? (Romans 9:22-24).

In this passage, Paul clearly gives two reasons why God endures wrongs with much longsuffering for a long time. First of all, when evil conditions are prolonged a long time, it gives God the judicial right to demonstrate the intensity of His wrath and the greatness of His power—expended upon the vessels of wrath. Paul said that God keenly intends to demonstrate to creation the full intensity of His wrath and power. He plans to pour this wrath upon "the vessels of wrath prepared for destruction." However, in order to show such levels of wrath and power, there must be a level of violation and injustice to deserve such a display of powerful wrath. So God endures the wickedness of the wicked for long periods of time because the greater their violations of His holy will, the greater the wrath He can justly demonstrate. In other words, the longer your adversary troubles you, the greater the wrath God can dispense upon him.

At the same time, the totally opposite dynamic is at work with regard to the vessels of mercy. In their case, God wants to demonstrate the fullness of His glory on their behalf. In regard to the righteous, the Lord says, "I want to show the entire created order the riches and power of My glory in the church, but if I intervene right now, I won't receive enough glory out of the thing. No, I want more glory than this. So I'm going to wait just a little bit longer until the circumstances give me the legal right to manifest the full intention of My glory on their behalf." In other words, the longer God waits to deliver you, the more glorious the salvation will be.

When God is in this mode of enduring and waiting, the righteous have only one way to live at such times—by faith. "'But the just shall live by his faith'" (Habakkuk 2:4, a verse whose context is the subject of waiting on God). Only true faith survives the wait. Anything less says, "My life is slipping away from me, I've got to do something different." Faith is willing to lose its life in the present, however, in order to gain its ultimately destiny.

GOD'S ACCELERATED PROGRAM

Another reason God will have you wait on Him is because He uses the waiting season to accelerate your learning curve.

When God wants to put you on the fast track, He brings everything in your life to a grinding halt. Everything stops, and all you can do is wait on Him. To do the quickest work in you, God waits. He puts you in His crucible, sticks you into the fire, turns the flame on high, and then says, "Wait on Me." There, in that place of intense heat and pressure, He will change you far more effectively than if there were no fire. Through the crucible, God can do a deeper and more comprehensive work within you in three years than in fifteen years with no pressure.

Waiting has a way of changing everything about you. I said to the Lord, "Okay, Lord, if You're so intent on changing me, go ahead and deal with the matter at hand. I realize You want to touch my pride. So let's stay on task and deal with my pride." I could imagine Him responding, "Yes, Bob, I'm going to deal with your pride. But I'm also going to visit a host of other issues in your soul at the same time." When God has us waiting on Him, He messes with every compartment in our being. He leaves no stone unturned. He starts at A and doesn't give up until He's made it all the way to Z.

But I complained, "Lord, this doesn't have anything to do with A or Z. You're dealing with P right now. You're after my pride. Deal with P, and then let's move on to Kingdom exploits." He came right back, "Oh yes, we'll take care of P, all right. But while we've got you here, let's go ahead and hit everything else while we're at it." He uses the crucible to change everything about you, that you might be conformed to the image of Christ. And how does He accomplish all this? Simply by bearing long with you.

God doesn't seem to be in quite the rush we are. He has taken an eternity to get to this point, and He knows He has an eternity ahead of Him. So if He takes, as in the case of Abraham, 25 years to birth your destiny, then what's the big deal? When you look at how God wrote the stories of His greatest saints—like Abraham, Jacob, Joseph, Hannah, Naomi, David, Jeremiah, and many others—one of the common denominators of their lives is how God took many years to craft and complete the story of their lives.

On one occasion, when I was keenly feeling both the duration and the pain of the wait, I asked the Lord to hurry up and finish His work in my life. That's when I heard, "I call fast boring." God is a good Author, and He likes a good plot. He's into dramatic flair, story lines with mounting tension, and climactic conclusions. He wants to build some suspense into your story, together with some intrigue, and a good splash of romance. By the time He's finished writing the story of your life, Joseph won't be the only one with a tale to tell. You'll also be able to say, "Let me tell you about the time…"

God doesn't measure your journey in days or weeks or months. He shapes the broad strokes of your life with a brush called "years." So when it seems that God is taking years to complete His work in your life, don't be alarmed or thrown off balance. Stay in the place of persevering prayer, and pace yourself for a lifetime of adventure with God.

ENDURING FAITH

Another reason God bears long with us is because of the powerful way endurance shapes and deepens our faith.

Jesus extolled persistence in prayer because He understood the power of enduring faith. The most powerful commodity in the Christian life is a genuine faith that perseveres through darkness and pain and refuses to relax its hold on God. I realize that's a very bold statement, so to explain it I want to direct you to what I consider to be the hardest verse in the Bible to obey.

My brethren, count it all joy when you fall into various trials, knowing that the testing of your faith produces patience. But let patience have its perfect work, that you may be perfect and complete, lacking nothing (James 1:2-4).

When James speaks of falling into various trials, he is not speaking of falling into moral sin (such as fornication or stealing), but falling, rather, into calamity or tragic circumstances. Trouble has a way of blindsiding our lives so suddenly that, when it hits, we feel like we've taken a "fall." It may come in the form of financial disaster; it may be something that separates us from a very dear relationship; or it may come in the form of an accident. There are so many ways we fall into various trials.

For instance, suppose you're walking outside in wet weather, and you're unaware of the slick spot on the pavement in front of you. Suddenly your feet go out from under you, you fall backwards, and your head lands on the pavement. BAM!

And then the verse comes to mind, "Count it all joy when you fall into various trials."

You're thinking, "I would like to count this fall a joy, but the fact is, my head is split open, blood is gushing, and I suddenly have a massive migraine." My point is, when you take a fall, there's nothing harder in that moment of searing pain than to "count it all joy." How can you be joyful when there is absolutely nothing joyful about the disastrous fall you've just taken?

The only way to count it all joy is by *knowing*:"*knowing* that the testing of your faith produces patience." To be joyful in the test requires knowledge. What must we know? That God has a purpose! When we *know* that God allows such calamities in our lives for strategic purpose, then we are empowered to continue in patience with joy.

James 1:2-3 supplies us with an excellent definition of patience. Patience is: faith sustained over time, in the midst of pain. When faith is sustained in painful circumstances for a long duration, it has a remarkable power to change the soul. That's why I'm suggesting that this kind of patience is the most powerful commodity in the Christian life. Scriptural patience carries within it the grace and power to make us "perfect and complete, lacking nothing." What a declaration! My soul wants to argue, "How could any single thing make me perfect and complete?" But the Scriptures won't back down from this claim. Patience (enduring faith) has the power to make us perfectly mature in Christ. Wow! Little wonder God sometimes bears long with us. He wants the power of patience to have a whack at us!

When God bears long with us, but we respond in faith and unrelenting prayer, that's what produces patience; patience produces profound character change; and character change is the thing that makes us dazzling and beautiful to Christ (see Psalm 45:11). We long to change so that we might be desirable to Him.

HOW LONG, O LORD?

When we're waiting on God, we often wonder how God views the wait. Does He look at our years of waiting through the lens of 2 Peter 3:8 and say, "With Me, a thousand years are as a day. So ten years of your life is like a blink of the eyelids to Me. You may think that ten years is a long time to wait, but from My perspective the wait has been very brief"?

No. God doesn't evaluate our years of waiting through that lens. He doesn't brush off our seasons of waiting as insignificant. I believe there's scriptural evidence that God views the length of our waiting season through the lens of what He felt as a Man who lived on earth. Jesus knew what it felt like, as a Man, to wait for 30 years before His ministry was released. So when we're waiting on Him, He empathizes with the intensity of the duration because He Himself experienced the same thing.

Upon what Scripture am I basing this opinion? I have in mind the time when Jesus healed the woman whose back had been bent over for eighteen years because of a spirit of infirmity. When Jesus healed her He said, "'So ought not this woman, being a daughter of Abraham, whom Satan has bound—think of it—for eighteen years, be loosed from this bond on the Sabbath?'" (Luke 13:16). Look at that little phrase, "think of it." The phrase is an interjection that communicates emphasis and weighty significance. In other words, Jesus was emphasizing the severity of this woman's wait. She had been afflicted for eighteen years, and when Jesus pointed to those eighteen years, He didn't blow them off as insignificant. Rather, as a Man who lived in the body and understood what it was like to live under the constraints of time, He expressed how long that period of time really seemed to Him.

My point here is this: When you've been waiting on God for a long time, God doesn't dismiss that with a wave of His hand and say, "Aw, that's nothing." No, He appreciates the fact that such a large portion of our human existence has been held in the grip of the adversary. He empathizes with the duration of our waiting times as a Man who has tasted of them Himself. He feels the pain of the length of your wait and sympathizes with your weaknesses (see Hebrews 4:15).

WAITING FOR GOD TO RISE UP

When you're waiting on God for justice, you'll be able to partner with Him much more effectively if you understand the delay that sometimes occurs between the time that God passes judgment and the time He rises up to implement that judgment. To say it another way, in phase one, He pronounces judgment on the injustice that has assaulted you; in phase two, He rises up in power to enforce that judgment. It's not until God rises up in enforcing power that you actually see the circumstances change.

David wrote about this dynamic when he offered a one-liner that has become one of my favorite prayers: "Rise up for me to the judgment You have commanded!" (Psalm 7:6). David wrote Psalm 7 at a time when an adversary, named Cush, had risen against him. In response to Cush's attacks, David cried out to his Judge for justice.

When David prayed, "Rise up for me," he was saying, "Lord, You know my enemy has done wrong by me. I recognize You have already passed judgment against him because the Word of deliverance has already issued forth from Your mouth. But nothing in my circumstances has changed! My adversary is still harassing me. He is not going to back off without a show of force. So I'm asking You to rise up in power, exercise Your authority, and enforce in the natural realm the justice that You have already decreed in the Spirit realm."

When the Bible speaks of God's rising up, it means He is stepping into action mode. He is implementing that which has been decreed. The prayer, "Let God arise," means, "Let the power of God be demonstrated here and now!"

There is a difference between authority and power. For example, when a policeman wants to arrest someone, some people will submit to arrest simply because of the authority of the policeman's uniform. But there are those for whom authority is not enough. They won't submit to arrest unless there's a show of power. Only when the policeman pulls out his revolver will they stop and submit to the handcuffs. And for those who won't submit to that, the officer may need to demonstrate his power by pulling the trigger.

The vilest enemies of the law will submit only to

power. Your adversary is no different. This was demonstrated on the occasion when Jesus commanded the legion of demons to come out of the demon-possessed man. Jesus uttered the word, but the demons did not leave immediately.[4] Why not? Because the adversary always wrestles to keep his footing. He never concedes territory without a fight. Authority is not enough for demons; they only respond to power. Jesus had to rise up and exert His power in order to cast the demons out.

The way Jesus delivered this man confirms that there is sometimes a delay or gap between the time that God speaks His intentions and the moment of actual deliverance. To the undiscerning, it can appear that God has not yet spoken. But the Word has already gone forth and is awaiting its fulfillment. Isaiah spoke about this dynamic.

> *"For as the rain comes down, and the snow from heaven, and do not return there, but water the earth, and make it bring forth and bud, that it may give seed to the sower and bread to the eater, so shall My word be that goes forth from My mouth; it shall not return to Me void, but it shall accomplish what I please, and it shall prosper in the thing for which I sent it" (Isaiah 55:10-11).*

The Lord likens His Word to rain or snow which waters the earth. The harvest does not immediately spring forth the moment the rain falls but will appear in due course. The Lord gives us strong consolation by assuring us that His Word will not become void and of no effect. Even if

---

[4] See Mark 5:8 and context.

justice is delayed, we should not be unsettled, for the fulfillment is most certainly on the horizon.

Jesus has been given all authority in heaven and on earth,[5] but that authority is over a rogue state—planet earth. His authority is defied and resisted. For Christ's Kingdom to advance, there must be demonstrations of power. That's why we pray, "Rise up for me to the judgment You have commanded!" We are asking Christ to rise up in power and enforce His authority over our adversary.

When God rises up, everything changes! Little wonder the prophet thundered his warning, "'Be silent, all flesh, before the LORD, for He is aroused from His holy habitation!'" (Zechariah 2:13). Zechariah was saying, "God has been waiting a long time to act, but He has now arisen to action. Be silent, all flesh, for our God is on the move!"

WHEN IT'S PARTLY YOUR FAULT

While you're waiting on God, a profound purification takes place. The prophet pointed to this when He wrote,

Do not rejoice over me, my enemy; when I fall, I will arise; when I sit in darkness, the LORD will be a light to me. I will bear the indignation of the LORD, because I have sinned against Him, until He pleads my case and executes justice for me. He will bring me forth to the light; I will see His righteousness (Micah 7:8-9).

---

[5] Matthew 28:18.

Micah was acknowledging that his fall into calamity was due, in part, to his own sinfulness. In response, he had devoted himself to radical repentance. Repentance had produced profound change in his life. Furthermore, Micah recognized that his sin had not disqualified him from God's justice. Even though he was partly to blame for his dilemma, he knew that God would decree justice for Him.

Micah was possibly drawing on the revelation God had given to David, who had written hundreds of years earlier, "Deliver me from all my transgressions" (Psalm 39:8). David was asking for more than simply forgiveness. He was praying, "Lord, deliver me from all the ramifications of my own sinful choices. I know I don't deserve such kindness, but I believe in Your love for me. I believe that You will deliver me not only from my enemies, but also from the consequences of my own foolish choices."

Here's my point: Don't think you're excluded from God's justice simply because you are partially responsible for what has come down on your head. It's true; you have sinned—as we all have. But God will deliver you from those transgressions. You are a candidate for justice! So lift your cry for justice and do not relent.

When God visits you with His justice, you won't be the only one who is surprised. Your adversary will be also. Jesus said,

"But know this, that if the master of the house had known what hour the thief would come, he would have watched and not allowed his house to be broken into. Therefore you also be ready, for the Son of Man is coming at an hour you do not expect" (Luke 12:39-40).

Think of the master in this parable as Satan (he is the master of his house, or "the god of this world") and the thief as Jesus. Jesus is planning to sneak up on Satan's turf as a thief, with the stated intention of plundering Satan's house. If Satan were to know the hour Jesus is coming to you, he would prepare accordingly. Instead, he misreads the long wait, interprets it as a sign of God's displeasure, and becomes distracted with other matters that appear more urgent. Jesus' visitation to your life will catch him off guard, and the Lord will take advantage of the surprise factor by exploiting your deliverance to maximum glory.

TWO TOKENS OF PURPOSE

When you've been holding to Promise for a long time, it can be very challenging to always "see" with clarity the purposes of God during the wait. Most of us have our moments of lost perspective. You may feel like a spiritual rollercoaster—vacillating between peaks of clear insight and valleys of fogginess. When you're weak and your vision is fuzzy, the enemy tries to take advantage of your vulnerability by bellowing in your ear, "You are forsaken and abandoned by God!" Reflexively, you begin to evaluate whether you have truly heard from God or whether you are delusional for thinking God will rescue you.

In that moment of uncertainty, there are two things to look for—two signs that indicate God is still with you and still working in your life: *preservation* and *favor*. God uses preservation and favor as comforting indicators that you have not taken a detour somewhere and lost your way with God. They assure you that God's purposes are still in force.

Watch, first of all, for *preservation*. When you are

in a prolonged test that is supervised by God, you will be amazed to look around and realize, "I'm still here! I thought I would be gone—finished—done in—kaput—history—lights out. But I'm taking a second look and realizing, *I'm still here!* The voice in my head tells me I've been knocked out of the race, but when I look around, I realize I'm still kicking. God is *preserving* my life."

> *He preserves the souls of His saints; He delivers them out of the hand of the wicked (Psalm 97:10).*

> *Oh, love the LORD, all you His saints! For the LORD preserves the faithful, and fully repays the proud person (Psalm 31:23).*

> *He guards the paths of justice, and preserves the way of His saints (Proverbs 2:8).*

Preservation is powerfully reassuring. That's why I frequently offer David's prayer of Psalm 16:1, "Preserve me, O God, for in You I put my trust." While there are many things I wish for Him to preserve in my life, my foremost request is, "Preserve my soul so that it doesn't collapse under the weight of the heartsickness." (Heartsickness naturally happens when your hope in God's Promise has been deferred a long time.) I have prayed, "Preserve my soul against the cancerous despondency that is constantly seeking to erode and incapacitate my soul. Preserve the strength of my heart so that I can continue to persevere in love. Preserve my witness from being reduced to a decaying mass of stinking rot. Preserve me, O God!"

Because of the duration of the wait, I am constantly

fighting decay in my soul. Death is at work in me (2 Cor-inthians 4:12), which has its positive aspects, but on the down side, death wants to lead to decay. So as long as death is working in me, I must constantly draw upon His life, lest the death turn to decay. Abiding in His life is the only preserving power I've got. I must ingest spiritual an-tioxidants every day, for cancer wants to take me over.

So the pursuit of abiding in Christ has become my full-time vocation. His life, flowing into me, is preserving me. And not only am *I* being preserved; the grace that is flow-ing through my life is also serving to preserve *others* who are waiting on God. Ah, once again my spirit is arising, and I can see it: God is preserving my soul! I am still on the upward way with God.

Second, watch for *favor*. When you continue to walk faithfully in the way of the Lord, you'll notice that your life is surrounded by tokens of favor. There may be some who still reject or reproach you, but in most directions you see evidences of God's favor on your life.

The enemy wants you to think you've been abandoned and forsaken, but instead you see signs of the Lord's fa-vor on every side. You're more fruitful than ever. He con-tinues to supply your needs. God is even giving you favor in the eyes of others. You're receiving favor from folks you thought would despise and exclude you. You are a living testimony to the truth of God's Word: "For You, O LORD, will bless the righteous; with favor You will surround him as with a shield" (Psalm 5:12).

The whole thing seems so surreal, because on the one hand you have an adversary who has risen against you and is seeking to bring you down; but on the other hand, the favor of God is surrounding you, shielding you, and thrilling your soul. Your heart is in incredible pain, and yet you are sampling the delights and pleasures of God. The time of testing is not yet over, but even so the favor of God is already on you and is becoming increasingly obvious to others.

Beloved, when you see preservation and favor at work in your life, take note. You are in a God warp. Preservation and favor are sending out little signals, "There's more going on here than meets the eye. God is up to something. He has a purpose in all of this. This is going somewhere. Your story is not yet finished."

Now, I'm not *satisfied* with preservation and favor. I'll never rest until God avenges me of my adversary. But in the meantime, I see indicators of preservation and favor, and they are encouraging me to continue to set straight paths for my feet.

He is able to give us more, because we waited, than if we had not had the season of waiting.

WORTH THE WAIT

I'm convinced that God's primary reason for bearing long with us is simply this: He is able to give us more, because we waited, than if we had not had the season of waiting. Here's one of the strongest Scriptures that bears that out:

Therefore the LORD will wait, that He may be gracious to you; and therefore He will be exalted, that He may have mercy on you. For the LORD is a God of justice; blessed are all those who wait for Him (Isaiah 30:18).

Isaiah says it boldly—God waits to fulfill His Promise so that He can be gracious to us. Grace comes to those who wait. When His grace finally impacts us in its fullness, we will be so glad He took us through the delay. We will see the delay as necessary training to prepare us for our destiny. Isaiah comforts those waiting on God with clarion assurance: "The Lord is a God of justice!" In other words, Isaiah is saying, "When you stand in faith and love for a long time, suffering the assaults of the adversary while God bears long with you, it is viscerally important to God that justice be rendered you. God will not violate justice by having you wait and then not answer you. In the end, the answer—and more—will most certainly come because, with God, nothing is more important than meting out justice."

This principle is central to the message of this book, so come to the next chapter as we expound it more fully.

7

RESTORATION AND RESTITUTION

Now there was a widow in that city; and she came to him, saying, "Get justice for me from my adversary" (Luke 18:3).

Jesus equipped us with seven power-packed words when He gave us the prayer, "Get justice for me from my adversary." You can't pray more dangerously and powerfully than when you're quoting Jesus. I always gravitate in my prayer life toward the prayers Jesus furnished because those are the prayers the Holy Spirit most delights to honor. Jesus gave it to you—use it! Pray the red![1]

When you take your stand before your Judge and cry incessantly to Him, "Get justice for me from my adversary,"

---

[1] I am referring to "Red Letter Edition" Bibles that have the words of Jesus highlighted in red ink.

you are offering what may be the most powerful prayer possible, because the cry for justice means you're asking for two things: restoration and restitution.

Restoration constitutes a return to original condition. Your enemy has come against you to steal, to kill, and to destroy. He has taken from you what is rightfully yours as a child of the King. When you cry for justice, justice demands a restoration of what was stolen. To satisfy justice, the Judge says to your adversary, "You must return what you took. Totally and completely." Justice will be satisfied with nothing less than full restoration.

However, if the enemy has stolen from you, and then God has borne l-o-o-o-o-o-o-n-g with you, another element plays into the equation. Not only have you been without that thing, but you've been without it for a l-o-o-o-o-o-o-n-g time. Now, you qualify not only for *restoration* but also for *restitution*. *Restitution involves punitive damages for losses sustained over time.* In other words, if you've been ripped off by your adversary for many years, justice demands that you be compensated for more than just the original loss (restoration); justice will not be satisfied until you are also compensated for the personal distress, inconvenience, and loss suffered due to the duration of the deprivation (restitution).

Restitution involves punitive damages for losses sustained over time.

Let me illustrate.

JOSEPH

Justice demanded restoration for Joseph. Restoration said, "Joseph has been wrongly imprisoned under false charges by Potiphar. He has been robbed of his freedom.

He must be restored to full liberty. You must release him from jail and clear his name and record."

Restitution piped up, "Wait a minute! If all you do is give Joseph his freedom back, you aren't satisfying all the claims of justice. Because Joseph was not only without his freedom; he was without it for a long time! He's been in that squalid Egyptian prison for *ten years*! He will *never* have a normal, brotherly relationship with Benjamin. There have been weddings and family festivities that he will *never* attend. A lot of water has gone under the bridge in ten years. There are countless events that can never be replayed or repeated. After all these years, Joseph has suffered lifelong losses that can never be repaid or made up. No, you must do more than just restore him to freedom."

Restitution necessitated, yea, demanded more. Restitution said, "Give Joseph the throne." Joseph qualified for the throne because justice required both restoration *and* restitution.

JOB

Restoration said, "Give Job his health back. This is wrong. He is a godly man, and he's been robbed—not only of his health, but also of his financial base and his ten beloved children. Justice demands that you renew his health, restore the flocks and herds he lost, and give him ten more kids."

Restitution spoke up, "Wait a minute! If all you do is give him ten more children and his health and herds, you're not answering the depth of trauma and horror this man has just endured. He has not only suffered intensely, but he's suffered for a long time. Don't even begin to suppose that giving him ten more kids will answer for the ten he's lost. Those were his cherished children, and now he'll never have them back. He has dangled between life and death for these many months; he has endured all kinds of relational chaos with his wife, his friends, and Elihu; he has wrestled through a theological meltdown; his mental, emotional, and physical suffering has been measureless. You've got to do more than just restore his losses."

Job suffered dearly. But now God was rising up to avenge His elect, and justice would require strong consolation. Restitution said, "Yes, you've got to heal Job and give him ten more children. But that's not enough. You've got to give him double his former wealth. But that's still not enough. You've got to give him the first book of the Bible." (Yes, the book of Job is the first Bible book actually penned, outdating even the book of Genesis in antiquity.) "But that's still not enough. You've got to give him a spiritual inheritance both in his generation and in every generation to follow. But that's still not enough. You've got to give him a revelation of God!"

Yes, beloved, there came a day when the whirlwind of God visited Job, the skies rolled back, and Job beheld the throne of God with the sons of God presenting themselves before Him. He saw the heavenly showdown between God and Satan, thus gaining understanding into the purpose of his trial. Speaking of this powerful encounter with God, he wrote, "'I have heard of You by the hearing of the ear, but now my eye sees You'" (Job 42:5).

Wouldn't *any* journey, no matter how painful or long, be worth going the distance if, as part of the attainments, you ended up beholding God Himself in His majestic beauty and glory? Can there be a greater reward than to be granted a first-hand revelation of the surpassing greatness of God? Is any price tag too steep to be given a face-to-face encounter with the risen Christ?

Restitution elevated Job to the most sublime heights of spiritual revelation and understanding.

ELIZABETH

Restoration said, "It's only just and right that Elizabeth be granted a baby. She has remained blameless before God and man all these years and has cried to heaven for a baby. She has not developed a bitter spirit because of her heartsickness, nor has she accused God of wrong. She continues to stand faithfully and affectionately before her God. Justice must be served. Give her a baby!"

Restitution countered, "Wait a minute! If you just give Elizabeth a baby, you're not answering all that this woman has endured. She has lived a lifetime of reproach, borne the shame of childlessness in a culture where barrenness is considered a curse of God, and suffered through gut-wrenching years of longing to be a mother. How many nights has she fallen asleep with her pillow wet from her tears? How long has she travailed in her soul for an answer from heaven, only to feel like the heavens are brass? No, you've got to do more than just give Elizabeth a baby. You've got to give her a baby *boy*. But that's still not enough. You've got to give her a *prophet*. But that's still not good enough. Elizabeth, you get *more than a prophet*—you get *John The Baptist*!"

SEVENFOLD RESTITUTION

The principle we're illustrating here is articulated clearly by Solomon:

*People do not despise a thief if he steals to satisfy
himself when he is starving. Yet when he is found,
he must restore sevenfold; he may have to give up
all the substance of his house (Proverbs 6:30-31).*

This proverb says that when the thief is brought to
justice, he must restore as much as sevenfold to his victim.
Similarly, when your enemy (the devil) comes to steal, kill,
and destroy, and then God bears l-o-o-o-o-o-n-g with you,
when God finally rises up to avenge you of your adversary
He will extract from him as much as a sevenfold return on
what was originally taken from you.

The devil wants you to believe that justice delayed
means justice denied (so that you will lose heart and give
up asking). But in fact, justice delayed means recompense
compounded.

Now we're starting to understand why God sometimes
bears long with His elect. Is it possible, beloved elect of
God, that God has called you to wait upon Him because He
wants to exact as much as a sevenfold return
from your enemy for the years he has stolen
from you? If God had given you immediate
justice, you would have simply received restoration. But now, because you have waited
this long for justice, you are a candidate for
restitution. Could it be that God has not yet
avenged you of your adversary because He
has more for you in this thing than you've ever thought or
imagined for yourself?

*Justice
delayed
means
recompense
compounded.*

Maybe God hasn't answered your prayer yet because
He *likes* you. Maybe it's because He's *chosen* you. Maybe
it's because He's chosen to catapult you onto the same
path that the greatest saints of all time have trodden. You'll

never touch what they touched without walking where they walked. The greatest potential of the Christian life is not found merely in the foothills of restoration but in the sublime tableland of restitution.

THE SCARS OF LOSS

We get excited at the prospects of sevenfold restitution, and yet let me emphasize that we reap this kind of dividend at a steep price. We don't qualify for restitution unless the loss has been severe, deep, and significant.

Stop for a moment, and consider with me the cost of qualifying for restitution. It means enduring many years of painful loss. And even though there is restitution, the reality of the actual loss is a scar that marks us forever.

Take, for starters, the indelible mark left upon Job because of the loss of his first set of ten children. Yes, he was changed, healed, restored, and given a second set of children. But nothing could erase the fact that he had lost his first children. They were forever gone, and their absence represented a hole in his heart that nothing could fill. This left an eternal scar on Job's soul. There was a certain pervasive sobriety that would never leave him because he carried this grief to his grave. This was the "limp" that he would never shake. The cross had left its mark on him. The greatest identification with the cross will always leave these kinds of scars, which are basically the unresolved griefs of irretrievable losses. The saint has been branded by the prison, and even after release, he carries the branding. Paul was delivered from many trials but carried in his body the marks of Jesus. Joseph was raised to the throne of the land and yet was robbed of a childhood relationship with his brother Benjamin. None of their attempts at relationship-building could produce that kind of familial camaraderie. There was a certain affinity that was forever absent in their relationship, and that pain was just one of many that attended Joseph for the rest of his life.

David, because of the wilderness years, forever lost his former relationship with Michal. She was the wife who once loved him but now despised him. It would have been different had the wilderness not been so prolonged.

Naomi was comforted with Obed's birth, but she never got her husband and two sons back.

Anna discovered a place of great authority in intercession, and yet she never married again.

Moses led his nation out of bondage, yet he never did get to enjoy a peer relationship with any of his people. He lost every friendship he had ever cultivated in the palace. Because God bore long with Moses in the wilderness of Midian for 40 years, he was not able to enjoy a Hebrew wedding, nor were his parents or siblings present to celebrate the occasion with him.

Abraham was assured that he would be a father of many nations, but because of the arduous journey to which he was called, he never really belonged anywhere. There was no place on earth that he could call home. Furthermore, he lost his relationship with Lot—the one relative who had walked the closest and longest with him. And then he was forced to send away his firstborn son, Ishmael. It's true that Abraham entered into great glory, but it's also true that he paid a price for it.

The point is: The losses are real, and the scars eternal. And yet, the suffering is worth it because of the glory which is revealed in us. After enduring through years of pain, you will look back on the affliction and call it "light," and you will describe the years as "but for a moment."[2] Why? Because you will see how they worked for you a far more exceeding and eternal weight of glory.

And the scars? They have value both in this life and in that which is to come. In this life, they grant the saint greater authority, they lend greater credibility to his witness, and they season his soul with meekness in the midst of abounding ministry effectiveness. In the life to come, they become the basis for profound affection with the Master. Even as we will caress His scars, He will caress the scars of those who shared in His cross and bear in their beings the same kinds of marks. The honor of bearing scars in that Day will be unparalleled.

So even though the scars represent significant pains, the restitution and intimacy in this age is profoundly rewarding, and the glory in the next age is exceedingly great. The losses are not worthy to be compared with the gains.

GOD CHANGES WHAT YOU ASK FOR

When you've been waiting on God for a long time, one of the things that changes during the waiting season is the nature of what you request of God. Early in the journey you might have been content with a lesser request, but now that you've endured all these years of heartsickness and grief, you're no longer satisfied with what you once desired. Now you want more.

Caleb's life is a marvelous illustration of this truth. Caleb was the man in the Bible who got a raw deal (or so I

---

[2] "For our light affliction, which is but for a moment, is working for us a far more exceeding and eternal weight of glory" (2 Corinthians 4:17).

once thought). He—along with Joshua—had faith the first time around to enter Canaan and take on the giants in the land. But because the other ten spies discouraged the entire nation from entering, Caleb had to do forty years in the wilderness with all the unbelievers.

I complained to the Lord about this, "Lord, that's not fair! Why should Caleb have to do forty years in the wilderness when he had faith to enter the land?" I figured there must be something more to the story that I wasn't seeing, so I looked at Caleb's story more carefully. Here's what I saw.

After Caleb had endured the forty dusty years in the wilderness and had conquered the land of Canaan together with his comrades, the time finally came for Joshua to assign to each man his inheritance. Each man was to get a field, or a house in a field, or a house on a city wall. When Caleb stepped forward to receive his inheritance, I can imagine him saying to Joshua, "I don't just want a house in a field anymore. I would have been happy with that 45 years ago, but now that I've endured these many long years through the wilderness, I want more. I want a whole mountain. Give me this mountain!"

I think God wanted to give Caleb a mountain all along. But God knew that if Caleb had been given a whole mountain on the first visit to Canaan, the entire nation would have been up in arms, aghast with envy. So I can imagine God thinking, "Caleb, I want to give you a mountain, but in order to do it in a way that the people will accept, you're going to have to do forty years in the wilderness. You'll experience scorpions, dust storms, and vipers. But if you'll endure to the end, the time will come when you will have the credibility with the people to ask for and to take an entire mountain for your inheritance."

By enduring the wilderness with patience, Caleb entered into sevenfold restitution.

When we endure a long wilderness walk, it has the same effect upon us it had on Caleb. The length of the journey changes the soul's aspirations. No longer easily satisfied with the lower foothills of grace, we now long to conquer the greater peaks of glory that God has made available to us.

At the beginning, your prayers have elements of selfishness and carnal desire woven into them. You don't realize it at the time, but the carnal ambitions of the heart are discoloring your requests. As you wait on God, He refines your passions and purifies your desires, until you are asking for those things that are truly upon His heart. In the persevering, all that is not of God is burned away, and that which remains is that which is impassioned by the heart of God. And at the end of the day you realize God had more in His heart for you than you had for yourself.

"But as it is written: 'Eye has not seen, nor ear heard, nor have entered into the heart of man the things which God has prepared for those who love Him'" (1 Corinthians 2:9).

8

THE SPEEDILY OF GOD

"And shall God not avenge His own elect who cry out day and night to Him, though He bears long with them? I tell you that He will avenge them speedily" (Luke 18:7-8).

In Chapter 6, we emphasized how God bears long with the elect. So now, as you read verse 8 above—"'He will avenge them speedily'"—you have a moment's pause. "Okay—uh, does God bear long with the elect, or does He avenge them speedily? Which is it? Does He wait a long time, or does He act quickly?"

Ah, we've finally come to the paradox[1] in the parable. This is the part of the parable that got many of our translators into trouble. They looked at the apparent

---

[1] A paradox is a seeming contradiction between two opposing truths, requiring divine insight to resolve it. Once understood, the paradox becomes the basis for profound insight into spiritual truth.

contradiction between verses 7 and 8, considered that
Jesus was too wise to contradict Himself, and for some
reason decided to change the wording. But I'm glad that
versions like the NKJV and KJV translate it accurately because now we are forced to wrestle with the paradox.

This isn't the first time, however, that this paradox is
articulated in the Bible. You may recall seeing these words
in Habakkuk, in reference to God's promised intervention:

> *Though it tarries, wait for it...It will not tarry*
> *(Habakkuk 2:3).*

So we're back to the same question. Does God's intervention tarry, or does it not tarry? Does God bear long
with His elect, or does He avenge them speedily? Which
is it??

The paradox within these statements is strong, and I
have only one way to resolve it. There is one
compelling truth that brings both sides of
the paradox together: *Sometimes God bears
l-o-o-o-o-o-n-g with His elect—in order to
avenge them speedily.* To say it another way,
sometimes God seems to take for-e-e-e-e-ver to
change everything speedily. You may wait on
God a long time, but when God finally choos-
es to act on your behalf, He will act decisively and change
everything dramatically and suddenly.

*Sometimes
God seems to
take forever
to change
everything
speedily.*

Habakkuk would have resolved the tension with the
same answer. I can imagine him saying, "Absolutely! Is this
supposed to be a new revelation? That's what I wrote centuries ago. When the Promise of God tarries, wait for it to
be fulfilled because there is coming a day when He will

fulfill His Promise. And when He does, there will be no further tarrying or hesitation or prolonging of the waiting season. Everything will change swiftly. And the dramatic nature of the change will be attributable to God alone, so all the praise will be His."

Sometimes God seems slow to respond to your prayers; but when He finally rises up and puts the thing into gear, fasten your seatbelt, you're in for a ride. Because when God finally steps into action, the thing is going to shake down and shake down *quickly*.

Some believers, after praying for something for a little while, will too hastily come to the conclusion, "Well, I guess I'm just not going to see the power of God manifest." So they give up asking. Jesus would use this parable to arrest our attention, "You've come to the wrong conclusion!" The wait doesn't mean God isn't going to answer; it simply means *He wants you to contend for far more than you were initially asking for*. Beloved, *now* is the time to contend for the supernatural! We must give ourselves to unrelenting prayer, without losing heart, until we uncover the speedily of God. Jesus is emphatic about the Judge's intention: "He *will* avenge you speedily!"

> The wait means He wants you to contend for far more than you were initially asking for.

Many times in the Bible, God called on men and women to wait on Him for extended periods of time (occasionally months, but more often years), during which time His promises seemed to be suspended or revoked. But then in the fullness of His plan, He opened a door and suddenly catapulted them into their destiny. This pattern of "wait a long time for God to change everything speedily" recurs very commonly in Scripture. One of the most delightful instances of this pattern is found in the story of Mordecai.

MORDECAI

Mordecai was a devout Jew who lived in exile in Susa, the capital city of Persia, together with many other Jews who had been forcibly relocated from the land of Israel. Although a captive, there came a time when he experienced a sudden turnaround in his fortunes. I am recounting this part of Mordecai's story because it shows that, when you step into the speedily of God, circumstances can change so quickly that your head starts spinning.

Mordecai had raised his cousin, Esther, in his household. She was exceedingly beautiful, and through a series of events had become queen in the land. So Mordecai adopted the practice of sitting at the king's gate each day so he could inquire into Esther's welfare.

Meanwhile, the king had promoted Haman the Amalekite to a place of favor in his kingdom. The king had commanded everyone to honor Haman, but Mordecai would not bow before him because he knew him to be an evil man. In revenge, Haman decided it wasn't enough to simply target Mordecai, so he devised a plot to exterminate *all* the Jews of the kingdom. The king signed Haman's decree, and the day was set when all the Jews would be killed.

Since the decree had already been made official legislation, Mordecai and the Jews were as good as dead. But Mordecai began to appeal to Esther in private, that she might intervene and beseech the king on behalf of herself and her people. Esther's efforts would prove successful, but that's not the aspect of the story I want to highlight here. For now, I want to focus on Mordecai's story to demonstrate "the speedily of God."

For years, Mordecai had been a captive in a foreign

land. But suddenly, through legislation enacted by an adversary, the plight of the Jews took an alarming downturn and a decree of death hung over their heads. Mordecai fasted and called upon God, together with his fellow Jews. And the day finally came when God tipped the domino, causing everything to change dramatically. Here's how it happened for Mordecai.

On a certain morning, he woke up in the king's gate, a dead man. (He was a walking dead man, for the day of his execution was already determined.) Then, early that morning, his great rival and enemy, Haman, walked up to him and said, "Uh, may I have a word with you?"

Haman proceeded to pull out one of the king's choice robes and, draping it over Mordecai's shoulders, said, "Excuse me, but the king insists that you wear this today." Then he motioned Mordecai over to the royal steed he had brought, saying, "Uh, Mordecai, would you please mount the king's horse? The king has commanded that you ride his horse today." So Mordecai got on the king's horse, wearing the king's robe, and then Haman began to promenade both horse and rider through the busy marketplaces, calling out loudly into the streets, "This is what the king does for the man whom he delights to honor."

Mordecai must have been one baffled man. Here was his archenemy, clothing him in a royal robe, escorting him on a royal horse, and heralding his praises throughout the citadel. As Mordecai was riding atop the horse, he was probably thinking to himself, "What is wrong with this picture?"

Then Haman dropped him back off at the king's gate and hurried to go to a banquet with the king and queen. It was at this banquet that Esther exposed Haman as the one who had devised the plot to exterminate her and her people. In fury, the king hung Haman on the gallows that Haman had just built the day before for Mordecai. Then Esther said, "May I introduce you to my cousin?" And she brought Mordecai into the presence of the king. At that, the king took off his signet ring of royal authority and placed it on Mordecai's finger.

So in one 24-hour period, Mordecai went from being a dead man in the king's gate to holding the signet ring of judicial authority for the entire kingdom. I call that "speedily!"

My soul says, "Lord, give me a day like that one!"

SPEEDILY, BUT NOT OVER IN A DAY

When God intervened on Mordecai's behalf, everything changed speedily for him. However, his 24-hour turnabout was only the beginning of his story. When God brought His salvation to Mordecai's life, it was manifest in several successive sequences of vindication and honor.

This pattern, experienced by many men and women in the Bible, still happens today. You may wait for the longest time for God to move, but when God finally steps into action, you are now in "the speedily of God." That does not mean, however, that all the changes will happen in a moment of time. More commonly, the salvation of God will unfold as a series of events or a succession of deliverances. To use seismological language, the initial earthquake may read 9.2 on the Richter scale, but that doesn't mean the activity is over; there may be several aftershocks that will continue to reverberate with God's justice.

God is too much into drama to be satisfied with one sudden KABOOM and then it's over.

God has taken a long time to get this angry with your

adversary, and His anger will not be placated with one sudden KABOOM and then it's over. He is too much into drama to be satisfied with a brief, momentary deliverance. There's been a whole lot of suspense and tension during the waiting season; now, there's going to be a correspondingly dramatic unfolding of Promise as God metes out vengeance upon your adversary.

True, God is slow to anger. But consider this: He's also slow to dispense His anger. But I'm getting ahead of myself. Let's start by meditating upon the first sentence: God is slow to anger.

One reason God bears long with His elect is because He is so slow in rising to full anger against the adversary.

The prophet Nahum spoke of this quality of God as it was manifest toward the Assyrians. The Assyrians had arisen against Israel, had conquered the Northern Kingdom of Israel (headquartered in Samaria), and had deported the people to Assyria. Then they rose up again to come against the Southern Kingdom of Judah (headquartered in Jerusalem). The Assyrians came against God's people in wave after wave of vicious assault, and although God's people cried out to Him for deliverance, God didn't seem to respond. On the surface it appeared that God had abandoned His people and no longer cared about their welfare. The prophet Nahum, however, was given divine insight into the heart of God. Here's what he wrote:

> *God is jealous, and the LORD avenges; the LORD avenges and is furious. The LORD will take vengeance on His adversaries, and He reserves wrath for His enemies; the LORD is slow to anger and great in power, and will not at all acquit the wicked (Nahum 1:2-3).*

Nahum assures the people that God is not indifferent to their plight. He is jealously protective of His beloved people, His Bride, and He is most certainly going to avenge Himself on the adversary that has risen against them. However, Nahum wants them to understand why it seems that God delays His responses. The issue, says Nahum, is that God is "slow to anger." He is not only slow to anger toward His people; He is also slow to anger toward their adversary.

When the enemy sweeps in and wreaks havoc among God's people, the elect begin to cry out, "Get justice for me from my adversary!" God's answer is: "I'm not angry enough yet to do anything about it." But the elect don't relent. They cry out day and night for vengeance. Weeks turn into months, but God is still saying, "I'm just not that angry yet." But the elect won't let go. They continue night and day, refusing to be silent or to lose heart. The months of harassment turn into years, and God says, "Okay, I'm starting to get a little angry now."

Sometimes it seems to take God forever to get angry. With every assault of darkness, however, the Lord's anger continues to mount.

In contrast, we humans tend to be quick to anger. But then again, we are also quick to dissipate our anger. We flare up in an instant, but then in a minute our wrath is totally spent and we're over it. And I can suppose God thinking, "Is that all the anger you're capable of? In a moment it's over?"

That's not how God works. It takes Him a long time to become fully angry over a certain injustice, but then it also takes Him a long time to fully expend His wrath against the injustice. It's taken Him a long time to get this angry; don't think this kind of wrath will be appeased with a quick bang. No, a sudden flash-in-the-pan will not suffice. There will now come wave upon wave of justice to the situation. First comes restoration and then comes wave after wave of restitution.

You may feel right now like God is slow in responding to your adversary. But remember this: When He does finally exercise His wrath, His rage against your adversary will not dissipate in a moment either. There will come many waves of vindication and retribution and vengeance.

FOUR KINDS OF WAVES

The point before us right now is that when the speedily of God comes to us, it will be manifest in wave upon wave of blessing. I want to illustrate that truth by showing how the speedily of God visited Abraham and Jacob with many successive waves of restitution. So hang tight, we're going to get to Abraham and Jacob in a bit.

But first, when I think about God's waves of restitution, I am reminded that they are preceded by three other kinds of waves. So let's back up a bit, and deal with all the waves that affect believers' lives.

I see four general kinds of waves in the Bible. There are waves of *affliction*, waves of *righteousness*, waves of *depression*, and waves of *restitution*. In your journey with God, while you're crying out for justice, it is quite likely that you will experience all of these waves.

Bear with me if we seem to follow a lengthy bunny trail for the next several pages. But if you're experiencing these waves, you won't feel like this is a digression at all. When the adversary rose up against the widow, she was ravaged by waves of affliction and depression. In other words, these waves are a normative part of the journey.

Calamity triggers waves of affliction; we answer with waves of righteousness; our souls are buffeted with waves of depression; and then the speedily of God comes to us in waves of restitution.

To work our way through the progression, let's begin with what the Bible calls waves of affliction.

WAVES OF AFFLICTION

Your wrath lies heavy upon me, and You have afflicted me with all Your waves. Selah (Psalm 88:7).

Deep calls unto deep at the noise of Your waterfalls; all Your waves and billows have gone over me (Psalm 42:7).

When you're in a season of trial, it can seem like the affliction crashes over your soul with wave after wave of breaking and crushing. You cry out to God, but no relief seems to come. You're aware that the enemy has his diabolical fingers in the mix, but you're also aware of divine purpose and sovereign oversight, so you conclude with the psalmist that the source of the trial is ultimately God.

When these waves of affliction are bearing down upon your soul, you feel the intensity of the refining process.

For You, O God, have tested us; You have refined us as silver is refined (Psalm 66:10).

This Scripture says that God sometimes refines His people like silver. Psalm 12:6 tells us that silver is subjected to a seven-step process of refinement. God puts you in the fiery furnace—and now wave upon wave of affliction tests your soul. The heat is dizzying. He searches every nook and cranny of your heart and soul. He seems to be tearing down and destroying everything that has been built in your life over the years. Nothing is off-limits to His searching gaze. After what feels like an eternity, He pulls you out of the fire and takes away the dross on the surface. You're thinking to yourself, "Wow, that was the most intense trial of my entire life! I had never imagined such heat and pressure! Whew, am I glad that's over." And then you hear the voice, "That's one." And back into the fire you go.

Seven seasons of refinement! We have a precedent for this in the life of Nebuchadnezzar who was tested of the Lord in a fiery furnace for "seven times."

"They shall drive you from men, your dwelling shall be with the beasts of the field, and they shall make you eat grass like oxen. They shall wet you with the dew of heaven, and seven times shall pass over you, till you know that the Most High rules in the kingdom of men, and gives it to whomever He chooses" (Daniel 4:25).

We don't know how long the "seven times" of Nebuchadnezzar's trial actually lasted. Some have supposed it meant seven years. Or it could have been seven seasons or cycles of trial. With God, a "season" can be shorter or longer than a year.

When God tests you seven times over, He's not doing anything with you that He doesn't do with Himself. Psalm 12:6 says, "The words of the LORD are pure words, like silver tried in a furnace of earth, purified seven times." In other words, God doesn't utter a word from His mouth without first giving it a sevenfold test. By the time a word issues from His mouth, it has been fully proven as bearing eternal weight. Everything in God's presence gets this kind of scrutiny. If God tests every word of His own mouth with seven fires, little wonder that when we—broken, weak, sinful people—come under His gaze, we are completely undone by the amazing intensity of His refining fires.

The assurance of Psalm 66 is that if He refines you seven times over, He will assuredly bring you out to rich fulfillment. You may endure seven waves of refinement, but it is so that He might answer it with a sevenfold restitution into dimensions of Kingdom fullness you would not otherwise touch.

WAVES OF RIGHTEOUSNESS

Okay, we all agree that the waves of affliction can be incredibly intense. Now let's turn to the second kind of waves in the Bible: waves of righteousness. Isaiah was the one through whom God spoke about them.

"Oh, that you had heeded My commandments! Then your peace would have been like a river, and your righteousness like the waves of the sea" (Isaiah 48:18).

This verse likens your righteousness to the waves of the sea. Even though you have been beseeching heaven for a long time, you have not let go your righteousness and integrity. You continue to live in holiness and to exercise yourself daily in small acts of kindness and mercy, despite

your pain levels. Each expression of kindness arises as incense before the throne of God, witnessing to your commitment to godliness. Even though you are under assault
from your adversary and it seems as though your Judge is
not hearing your cries for justice—even so, you never relent or turn from clothing yourself in "the righteous acts
of the saints" (Revelation 19:8).

How does God view these acts of righteousness? To
Him, they are like ocean breakers crashing on the shore.
The fact that your present distress cannot move you from
practicing righteous deeds pounds the shores of heaven
like waves of a billowing sea. Standing one day on a Cali-
fornia beach and watching the waves break on the shore,
I observed three characteristics of waves: They are *incessant*, they are *thunderous*, and they are *impacting*.

Incessant: Like the waves of the sea, your godliness is
never-ending. Even though you're in warfare that you don't
totally understand, you continue to perform unremitting
acts of goodness. Everywhere you turn and with everyone
you meet, your life is a nonstop sequence of small tokens
of kindness dispensed in graciousness and mercy. A kind
word, a warm embrace, a gift to a needy person, a word of
encouragement, a soft answer in the face of wrath, an act
of fairness... Over and over, unceasingly, throughout the
day, your acts of righteousness are like waves of the sea.
They never stop.

Thunderous: Ocean breakers are explosive in sound as
they crash upon the shore. Similarly, your righteousness
crashes on the shores of heaven's awareness with thunderous volume. One tiny act of kindness is like a deafening roar before the courts of your Judge.

Impacting: When ocean breakers crash on the shore,
you can feel the ground shudder beneath your feet. In

the same way, your acts of righteousness move the very
pillars of God's temple. Although the winds of adversity
are blowing in your life, you refuse to abate your lifestyle
of righteousness and it moves heaven to its very foundations.

Not only are your incessant cries appearing before your
beloved Judge, but your incessant righteousness is a living
memorial that mounts to heaven and witnesses thunderously to your devotion and love. No device of darkness
can successfully silence the witness of your righteous life.
The impact in heaven is deafening and incessant, moving
the heart of your Judge. The roaring witness of your waves
of righteousness will inevitably be answered by God.[2]

Never surrender your righteousness!

WAVES OF DEPRESSION

Even though we respond with waves of righteous acts,
the reality is that when waves of affliction are allowed to
be loosed against us, they often trigger waves of depression in the soul. We have been warned in Scripture that
the intensity of spiritual warfare is going to increase in
the last days;[3] as it does, more and more believers will experience these waves of depression. Because of my own
battles with depression, I write this section out of a deep
care for those who know this struggle.

When God's saints go through seasons of intense trial

---

[2] Read the story of Cornelius in Acts 10 for an example of a man whose
righteous acts of giving to the poor rose before God as a veritable memorial. Moved by the memorial of Cornelius's almsgiving, God visited
him with an outpouring of the Holy Spirit that would reach ultimately
to every nation of the earth.

[3] Revelation 9 & 12; 1 Timothy 4:1.

and adversity, there are typically two responses happening simultaneously within them. On the one hand, because the saint is living in the Word and abiding in Christ's love, he (or she) is experiencing profound insight into the heart and personality and purposes of God in the trial; on the other hand, because the saint is a weak human being who is still living in the body, he is also susceptible to turbulence and distress in his soul. When you add the tormenting thoughts with which the enemy is actively attacking, it means that the saint has moments of frailty during which the soul is greatly vexed and in extreme duress. Feelings of loneliness and depression arise like ocean breakers, seeking to bury the soul in despondency and purposelessness.

Sometimes we respond to the furnace of affliction like an overcoming saint of God who is walking in the Spirit; but then we all have those moments when we feel the frailty of our flesh and the limitations of our humanity. At such times, depression and loneliness become tools in the hands of our adversary to press us deeper into our "cave of Adullam."[4]

I never had a depressed day in my life—until the summer of 1992 when all hell broke loose in my life. Suddenly I found myself being swept up in emotions that I previous thought a Christian should never experience or tolerate. My theology got washed overboard as the waves crashed over my soul.

I remember once, as a pastor in my mid-30s, attempting to address the issue of depression to my congregation on a Sunday morning. Never mind the fact that I had

---

[4] See 1 Samuel 22:1. The cave of Adullam was one of the places David lived during the years he was being hunted by Saul.

never wrestled with that monster myself, I was going to do my best to help my congregation deal with its tentacles. Now, after having drunk deeply of that cup, I shudder to think what my congregation heard that day. I have since imagined the Lord thinking to Himself, "So you want to be able to address the topic of depression with authority, do you? Well, in that case, let's put you in circumstances that will provide you with the opportunity to gain first-hand revelation." Whether the Lord actually looked at it in that fashion, I don't know. But I do know that I have been allowed to stand on the battleground of depression and experience this warfare for myself.

I'm going to share briefly about my own personal struggles with depression. As I do so, I am aware that it is a multi-headed monster, coming to different people in different ways, so that the causes and effectual responses are different with each person. I am fully aware that there is no single, all-inclusive answer for depression. So I don't share my experience with some sort of naïve expectation that one answer fits all. Rather, I simply share my own experience for it to be taken as just that—one person's journey in a still-unfolding victory over depression.

I now understand what Paul meant when he said we "wrestle" with principalities and powers (Ephesians 6:12). When battling depression, you are literally face to face with your enemy, in hand-to-hand combat, inhaling the stench of demons' breath as you fight for survival. One moment you feel like you're in a headlock, the next moment you're aware of grace that is empowering you to overcome.

At times I've felt like I've had demons dancing on my brain. It has seemed to me that two dark angels have been assigned to my life, to harangue me with an unending barrage of hopelessness and despair. The design of darkness has been to cause me to lose heart, to abort my pursuit of divine purpose in the trial, and to give up crying to my Judge day and night. I have chosen to believe that the intensity of the spiritual oppression is itself indicative of the significance of the battle and the glorious redemption God has in store.

I have a passion to help believers who struggle with depression because I've experienced it. I know how its winds blow through the soul, seeking to press your face into the mud and suck every ounce of faith and hope from your spirit. I hate depression! I intend to do warfare against this terrible tactic of darkness for the rest of my life.

On one occasion, as I was in the thick of battling a cloud of depression, I came upon these verses in my Bible reading:

> *If any of you lacks wisdom, let him ask of God, who gives to all liberally and without reproach, and it will be given to him. But let him ask in faith, with no doubting, for he who doubts is like a wave of the sea driven and tossed by the wind. For let not that man suppose that he will receive anything from the Lord; he is a double-minded man, unstable in all his ways (James 1:5-8).*

Well, here I was, with the winds of depression blowing at gale force, and if ever I felt like a wave of a sea, it was then. The winds were powerful, and my soul was being battered and tossed about. I was desperate for a touch from Christ, for I knew if I could but touch the hem of His garment, I would be healed. But now, as I felt tossed about by the winds of depression, this portion of Scripture was telling me that I was a double-minded man, unstable in all my ways, and I should not suppose that I will receive anything from the Lord. But that's why I was there, devoting my life to the Word and prayer, because I was desperate to receive from the Lord!

I was depressed before my Bible reading that day, but after reading the Bible I was *really* depressed!

I desperately lifted my cry to God, "God, is this verse describing me? Am I a double-minded man? Will I never receive anything from you?" I knew I was being tossed by the wind, but was I double-minded? The question was twisting my soul with pain. I had to have an answer.

Here's the answer that seemed to come. "No, Bob, this verse is not describing you. You are not a double-minded man. You are a single-minded man, for you have set your eyes on Me and Me alone. You refuse to look to any other saviors or sources of relief. You have fastened your gaze on Me only with a singular focus. You may feel like a wave of the sea right now because the winds of depression are blowing so strongly in your soul. But since I am the only One you seek, you are not double-minded. You have made Me your only source of salvation, and you still qualify to receive what you are asking of Me."

Then it came to me like this: "You can be a wave, or you can be a boat." A wave is tossed about by the wind, but a boat will harness the power of the wind and beat the storm. When a sailboat is facing contrary winds and seeking to forge ahead into the wind, sailors will set the sail in such a way as to harness the strength of the wind and use that power to drive into the very storm coming against them.

Have you ever seen a sailboat out on the waters on

a windy day that is leaning so far over on its side (called "heeling") that it looks like it's on the verge of taking on water, or tipping right over into the sea? The reason it's heeling at such a sharp angle is simple: It's heading directly into the wind. Well, technically speaking, a sailboat cannot head *directly* into the wind; the closest tack the helmsman can hold the boat at is a 20-degree angle. So the boat will go 20 degrees to the left, then 20 degrees to the right, and thus it will zigzag its way into the headwind. The more directly it attempts to head into the wind, and the stronger the winds, the harder it leans.[5]

So what do I do when the winds of depression come against me and seek to blow me about or bury me in despair? I set a sail. I harness the power of the winds of depression. I use the energy of those winds to press me into the Word of God and prayer in an impassioned pursuit of the heart and mind of Christ. I've been in this battle long enough to know the true source of light and hope. It comes when a living word from God, enlightened by the power of the Holy Spirit, is administered to the heart. When living understanding into the Word of God is granted to the heart by the power of the Holy Spirit, the clouds of depression move asunder and the light of God's hope and confidence begin to fill the soul of the battered saint. It is the administration of the living Word of God to the human spirit that is the antidote to depression. Man does not live by bread alone but every Word that proceeds from the mouth of God. When that Word comes from His mouth, you know that you will live again.

So when I'm depressed, I do like Jesus—I pray. It says

---

[5] Song of Solomon 5:8 shows how the Lord wants us leaning on Him, dependent upon on Him for every move we make.

of Jesus, "And being in agony, He prayed more earnestly" (Luke 22:44). When Jesus was hurting, He prayed; and when He was *really* hurting, He *really* prayed. So when I'm depressed, I redouble my commitment to prayer and to meditating in the Word. And when I'm *really* depressed, I get totally violent with my priorities. Everything else must go! The computer, the media, the TV, Christian books and magazines—everything must be pushed out of my way. I become a desperate man with tunnel vision. All I have room for on my hard-drive, other than the absolute necessities of daily obligations, is the Word and prayer. I use the depression to press me into the face of Christ. And I am of the persuasion that the answer to every dilemma is to be found in the face of Christ. If the answer is not to be found in Christ, then I have no Gospel to preach.

My cure for depression is to seek the Lord until He gives a living Word from His mouth that breaks open the clouds and releases the confidence of His purposes.

I love this little verse from Proverbs:

> *There are three things which are too wonderful for me, yes, four which I do not understand: The way of an eagle in the air, the way of a serpent on a rock, the way of a ship in the midst of the sea, and the way of a man with a virgin (Proverbs 30:18-19).*

My focus is on the third item in the list, "the way of a ship in the midst of the sea." It's an amazing wonder to behold a ship sailing in the turbulence of stormy seas. As the boat heaves in the water and comes crashing down on its hull, you begin to wonder how the boat could even survive. Surely it will be broken to pieces! And even if it's not destroyed, you think to yourself, there is no way the boat is ever going to get anywhere in this storm.

I remember once watching a sailboat from the shore as it was plowing into a strong headwind. I was measuring the boat's position against a landmark on the shore, and it appeared at a casual glance that the boat was making no progress whatsoever against the contrary winds. I thought to myself, "That boat's not going anywhere!" But then I came back to it a few minutes later, and thought to myself, "Wait a minute. I think that boat has actually moved." So I watched it carefully from my observatory, and sure enough, the boat was slowly crawling forward, using the power of the wind to drive into the storm.

My point is this: When you're in the battle of depression, and you're using the winds of depression to press violently into the Word and prayer, it doesn't look to a casual observer like you're going anywhere. To others, it looks like you're stuck. True, you're not setting any speed records right now. But hey, you've got a huge storm whipping you in the face! You're taking on gale-force winds! You're taking the pounding of your life. You may not be going anywhere *quickly*—but you *are* making progress. Your progress may not win any awards, but you're not giving up or losing heart. You are continuing daily in the Word and offering unrelenting prayer. And you're inching your way forward in the fiercest gale you've ever experienced.

To an observer, it looks like you're going to take on water any moment and capsize. Somehow, though, you stay afloat. It truly is a wonderful thing to behold: The way of a saint who has set a sail in the face of contrary winds, whose life is being battered by the stormy waves, and whose hope of making progress appears grim at best. But beloved, you refuse to lose heart! You continue to lean hard on Jesus. You continue to inch your way forward in the Spirit. And here's the amazing part: Not only are you going to survive this storm, and not only are you going to make progress—you are actually going to make it to your destination! And when you do, my, what precious cargo you will unload. You will deliver a rich deposit of grace and faith that was purchased in the greatest storm of your life.

The way of a saint (ship) in the midst of the rolling seas of depression? It is too wonderful, beyond understanding. It is a glowing tribute to the manifold grace of our glorious Redeemer.

WAVES OF RESTITUTION

The fourth kind of waves are waves of restitution. First came the waves of affliction. The adversary ripped you off, God bore long with you, and during the wait you cried out, "All Your waves and billows have gone over me" (Psalm 42:8). You felt His waves of reproach and discipline and forsakenness and refining. And what was your response? The entire time you were unrelenting in offering small acts of righteousness to the Lord, which crashed on the shores of heaven as thunderous breakers of righteousness (Isaiah 48:18). You faced the waves of depression and learned to harness the power of the winds in order to move forward in destiny in the midst of the storm. But now come breakers of another sort—the waves of restitution. Now you will be impacted by God's waves of vindication, salvation, deliverance, and honor.

As I said earlier, when God comes to visit your life with restoration and restitution, the restitution does not come in one sudden bang that explodes and then is over. It took God a long time to get this angry at your adversary, and His wrath will not be satisfied with one brief moment of restitution. No, His restitution will now visit your life in wave after wave of glory and honor and vengeance.

Again, the scriptural principle I'm invoking here is found in Proverbs 6:30-31.

People do not despise a thief if he steals to satisfy himself when he is starving. Yet when he is found, he must restore sevenfold; he may have to give up all the substance of his house.

You've known the waves of affliction, as many as seven seasons of refinement and purifying. How did you answer those seven seasons of breaking and crushing? With your own waves of righteousness. And now God has an answer for the seven seasons of crushing you faithfully endured. He now has seven seasons of restitution for you. This is your sevenfold return for what the thief stole. The restitution will visit you again and again. You're a vessel of mercy, and you're headed for glory!

ABRAHAM

I want to show you how God's salvation comes in wave after wave of restitution, and I know no better place to start than to go to the father of the faithful, to father Abraham. Abraham was given a Promise of a miracle baby when he was 75 years old, but as he and his wife, Sarah, continued to age, the possibility of the Promise becoming a reality appeared dimmer and dimmer. Sarah was already barren, but then the day came when she was too old to get pregnant. She was past her childbearing years. Her womb was twice dead.

During those years of aging, as Abraham and Sarah were pummeled by waves of affliction and waves of depression, they continued to respond to the Lord with their own waves of righteousness. Eventually the Lord would answer with His waves of restitution. Here's how it happened.

When Abraham turned 99, it was as though a switch was flipped in the Spirit realm. God rose up to visit Abraham with His salvation, and once the action started, it all began to shake down *speedily*. It's interesting that one year in Abraham's life—from age 99 to 100—takes up five whole chapters in the book of Genesis. Abraham had endured 24 years of seemingly zero spiritual activity, but God tipped the domino when he turned 99, and the fulfillments of Promise began to tumble.

First wave: God changed his name from Abram to Abraham. The name change was significant because of the meaning of Abraham's new name, "Father of a Multitude." Even though he still didn't have his miracle baby, Abraham was given a name in keeping with the inheritance God had prepared for him. Abraham was the first person in the Bible whose name God changed, but he wasn't the last. Every time God changed people's names, it was to help them rise to the potential of their God-ordained destiny. The new name was in itself a prophetic declaration of purpose and Promise.

Second wave: God gave Abraham the covenant of circumcision. The Creator of the universe made an unbreakable covenant with Abraham, a covenant that is still in force. This covenant will be manifest in fullness in the lives of ethnic Jews before the story of mankind is finished because the gifts and callings of God are irrevocable (Romans 11:29). This covenant with Abraham became the mainstay of the identity and hope of Abraham's offspring. Suddenly Abraham found himself with a new name and a covenant with God, and God was only beginning to unfurl His waves of restitution.

Third wave: God vindicated Abraham before those who had reproached him. I am referring specifically to Abraham's nephew, Lot, and the reproach with which Lot had reproached Abraham. Let me remind you of Lot's story.

Abraham took Lot under his wing when he moved from Haran to Canaan, no doubt largely because Lot's father had passed away. He became like a father to Lot, providing generously for him, so much so that Lot got established in his own personal momentum of material abundance. Lot developed his own flocks and herds and servants to the point of becoming independently wealthy under Abraham's protective blessing. But when Lot became strong and self-sufficient, that's when the problems began.

Strife began to develop between Lot's and Abraham's herdsmen, so they mutually agreed to separate and put some distance between their two households. That would quell the strife over feeding grounds. But before the separation happened, something turned in Lot's heart, and he became upset with Abraham. Genesis 13:8 indicates that a personal rift developed between Abraham and Lot, and Abraham was distressed that it had come to that. Lot seemed to have lost the perspective that all his fortune was due to Abraham's benevolence. Living in Abraham's household, he had come under divine blessing. When Lot moved, he didn't realize he was stepping away from his source of blessing. Nor did he realize that God was displeased with the reproach he had harbored in his heart toward Abraham. Instead of being grateful, Lot had become irritated and disgruntled.

Even after their parting of ways, Abraham continued to reach out to Lot. He fought a cadre of kings in order to rescue Lot from their grip. Then, when God determined to overthrow the cities of Sodom and Gomorrah, Abraham interceded on Lot's behalf so that he might not be destroyed. Abraham's heart remained noble and gracious toward Lot, but Lot was never able to recover from the offence he had harbored toward Abraham.

In Abraham's 100th year, while God was bringing restitution to his life, it's as though God were saying to Abraham, "Abraham, I know your heart toward Lot is pure, and I know you have prayed fervently for his blessing and prosperity. But I have noted the manner in which he has reproached you to those in his household, and I am resolved to vindicate you before him." So it was in the course of that year that Lot lost almost everything dear to him—his flocks and herds, his servants, his wife, and all his children except for two daughters. At the end of the day Lot was holed up in a cave with his two daughters, stripped of all his former abundance, ashamed and destitute. He could have returned to Abraham's household at that point, but his pride wouldn't allow it. Instead, he went to his grave in reproach and impoverishment.

Meanwhile, here came God's fourth wave of restitution to Abraham—a miracle baby! The Promise was fulfilled, and Abraham held precious little Isaac in his arms. He had a new name, a covenant with God, vindication before his detractors, and the fulfillment of Promise. And all four waves crashed upon his soul in one single, momentous year.

But God still wasn't done. The waves of restitution

would continue to visit Abraham, even for years to come. The day would come when, because of Abraham's willingness to sacrifice his only son on an altar to God, God would say to him, "By Myself I have sworn, says the LORD, because you have done this thing, and have not withheld your son, your only son—blessing I will bless you, and multiplying I will multiply your descendants as the stars of the heaven and as the sand which is on the seashore; and your descendants shall possess the gate of their enemies. In your seed all the nations of the earth shall be blessed, because you have obeyed My voice'" (Genesis 22:16-18).

Wow, talk about sevenfold restitution! God just kept on pouring it on, again and again. Oh the delight in God's heart to vindicate His beloved servant and lift him up from the pits of barrenness onto the mountains of fruitfulness. When God set His heart to bring restitution to Abraham, He did not relent until He had speedily answered the years of heartache with seven waves of restitution.

JACOB

I've just got to talk about Jacob right now because Jacob was another man who experienced the speedily of God, together with God's waves of restitution. But he first experienced the other kinds of waves ever before he saw restitution. Jacob was a man who could have penned those words, "all Your waves and billows have gone over me" (Psalm 42:7), for his was a life of sadness and grief. In fact, he himself summarized his life with these words, "'Few and evil have been the days of the years of my life'" (Genesis 47:9). He called his days evil because the vast majority of his life was characterized by sorrow and affliction.

From the start he knew that his father favored his brother, Esau. Then, because he deceived his father into giving him the patriarchal blessing, Jacob was hated by Esau. From that moment, Esau waited for an opportunity to kill him. So Jacob fled to his uncle Laban in Haran, where he was cheated and swindled by Laban. Tensions grew to the point where Jacob knew he needed to flee from Laban and return to his father in Canaan. He faced Laban's wrath for sneaking away from him, and then he prepared to face his brother's wrath. Next, as though that weren't enough, God put his hip out of joint, causing Jacob to limp awkwardly and painfully from that day onward. But his trials were far from over. The greatest trial of his life was about to be launched when his favorite son, Joseph, would be taken from him, presumably destroyed by a wild beast.

After Jacob lost Joseph, we know nothing about the next 22 years in Jacob's life because the biblical account is distracted with telling us Joseph's story in Egypt. When we are finally brought back to Jacob, we find him at age 130 in the grip of an agonizing drought. The famine was so severe that many regions were on the brink of starvation, Canaan included. When the report was broadcast that Egypt had grain for sale, Jacob sent his ten sons to go shopping for food (he kept Benjamin at home because with Joseph gone Benjamin was the only surviving son of his beloved Rachel).

When the brothers got to Egypt, the main man in Egypt suspected them of being spies. He imprisoned Simeon as surety, and sent the other brothers home with their food purchases and specific instructions that they were not to see his face again unless they brought their youngest brother back with them. When they arrived home without Simeon, Jacob was heartbroken. But he was absolutely devastated when he learned they couldn't buy any more food unless Benjamin was to go to Egypt with them.

Jacob said to his sons, in so many words, "Do you suppose I will allow Benjamin to go with you back to Egypt? Over my dead body!" I can imagine his sons replying, "Well, Papa, it just may be over your dead body. Because this famine is unrelenting, and the food we bought in Egypt has now been consumed. We must go back, or we will all die. You must release Benjamin to come with us."

It was the last thing Jacob wanted to do, to release Benjamin. But he had little choice because of the interminable famine that was sucking the life out of his children and grandchildren. If he clung to Benjamin, he lost; if he released Benjamin, he lost. He was in a lose-lose situation. And worst of all was the realization that God Himself seemed to be opposing him. (Jacob knew that God was sovereign over the weather, so the famine had to mean divine displeasure.) Heaven was against him (the famine); the main man in Egypt was against him (the Egyptian lord); and all of hell seemed to be against him (spiritual oppression). Trapped on all sides, Jacob lifted his gut-wrenching cry to the sky, "Everything is against me!"[6]

Let me point out that by now, after having walked with God for so many years, Jacob was a seasoned, mature saint of God. And yet he had zero insight into the future! He couldn't see past his nose. He had no idea that in roughly a month's time everything would turn around speedily. Jacob's blindness should comfort those who have heard the enemy's accusation, "You've been with the Lord long enough that surely by now you should be

---

[6] Genesis 42:36, New International Version.

able to see where God is taking you!" Jacob's life at 130 illustrates that sometimes even the most mature saints have moments when they are totally blind to what God has planned for them.

Unabated pressure from the famine finally forced Jacob to allow Benjamin to accompany the brothers back to Egypt to get more food. He offered a prayer to God for mercy, and then released Benjamin with the words, "'If I am bereaved, I am bereaved!'" (Genesis 43:14). Jacob's life was out of his control, and he was compelled to surrender to his worst nightmare—losing Benjamin. But even so, Jacob did not curse or turn away from His God. He prayed to his God and then released his son. He offered his waves of righteousness right to the end.

Little did Jacob know that within the month God would turn his fortunes and commence visiting Jacob with waves of restitution. Once the speedily of God was launched, restitution came tumbling down upon Jacob's soul in wave after wave of honor, goodness, and blessing.

First wave: About 25 days later, Jacob lifted his eyes to the horizon and lo, a veritable caravan was approaching his place. He looked and nearly lost it when he saw his beloved Benjamin waving joyfully to him. Then he heard him calling, "Papa, Simeon is freed from prison and has come home with us!" Then all the sons said, "Papa, sit down, we have some very special news to share with you. Papa, are you ready to hear this? *Joseph is alive!* He is alive and well. And not only is he living in Egypt, he is *running* Egypt! He is the main man over the entire Egyptian harvest!" In the first wave of restitution Jacob's sons were all restored to him.

Second wave: "Papa, look at all the food we brought back with us! All of this is a gift from Joseph."

Third wave: "Papa, Joseph insists that we all come down to him in Egypt. He said he will provide food for our households during the five remaining years of famine, and he will give us all free housing in the land of Goshen."

Fourth wave: Jacob was transported to Egypt in the equivalent of a limo. It was a padded carriage that sat atop a camel. It was the most dignified mode of transportation of that day, so Jacob rode into Egypt like a king.

Fifth wave: After getting settled in Goshen, Jacob came with several of his sons into the presence of Pharaoh, where he vested Pharaoh with a spiritual blessing (and without doubt the lesser is blessed by the greater).

Next wave: Jacob had the privilege of laying hands upon Joseph's sons and blessing them. Then he had the honor of prophesying over each of his twelve sons.

Seventh wave: After his passing, Jacob was given the funeral of the century. He was embalmed by the Egyptians and carried to Canaan by a regal procession of dignitaries and luminaries. Joseph and his sons buried him with style and honor. "Precious in the sight of the LORD is the death of His saints" (Psalm 116:15).

When I consider how the Lord visited both Abraham and Jacob with wave upon wave of restitution, my heart is deeply stirred. Truly He is still the God of Abraham and of Isaac and of Jacob.

CONTEND FOR A LIVING TESTIMONY

It is in this context that I wish to frame this portion of Hebrews:

Remember those who rule over you, who have spoken the word of God to you, whose faith follow, considering the outcome of their conduct. Jesus Christ is the same yesterday, today, and forever (Hebrews 13:7-8).

The writer of Hebrews encourages us to look at the outcome of the conduct of our spiritual leaders and be empowered to follow their example of faith. We can look at men like Abraham and Jacob, be inspired by how their stories conclude, and follow their faith. However, Hebrews is not asking us to look back to saints like Abraham and Jacob; it is asking us to look at our own contemporaries, the leaders who serve and speak the word of God to us now. We should be able to look at the outcome of the conduct of today's leaders and gain such encouragement that we are empowered to imitate their quality of faith.

Beloved, if there's anything the body of Christ needs today, it's mothers and fathers in Israel who have walked a journey in God, who have persevered in godly conduct and bold faith, and have attained the speedily of God. If God is fashioning you into one of those mothers or fathers, and you are on a spiritual journey with God, never let go God's Promise. Hold to it, persevere in faith, and press through the waves of affliction until you uncover God's waves of restitution.

Jesus Christ is the same yesterday, today, and forever. The Jesus who empowered Abraham and Jacob to press through their sorrows and gain restitution is the same Jesus today. He has not changed. He will empower you to endure the waves of depression and to answer with waves of righteousness until you experience God's waves of restitution. May the outcome of your conduct be a shining light in an evil generation that demonstrates the speedily of God and the greatness of His salvation!

9

THE SHAME OF REPROACH

If you're still waiting for the speedily of God to come to your life, then chances are pretty good that you will experience reproach for the "in-betweenness" of where you're at right now. There is no reproach for those who have reached their destination, but only for those who are still in process.

When you suffer loss but then God bears long with you, it's almost inevitable that you will feel shame. Reproach accompanies loss as surely as tears accompany sorrow. Widowhood, barrenness, restriction, affliction, bankruptcy—the shame we feel from these kinds of losses is very real. I want to devote an entire chapter to the shame of reproach because it is not only virtually universal in experience, it also can be almost overwhelming in its unanticipated intensity.

Reproach is a prominent biblical theme, discussed widely and comfortably by a broad range of biblical writers who felt its pain. But it's not always acceptable to talk about it among our friends. It is glaringly absent from the topics covered in most Christian conferences today. When reproach is not acknowledged as a valid element in the pilgrim's journey, its sting is all the more acute. I say it's time to demystify the subject and talk about it.

The widow of our Luke 18 parable would have been well served to be comforted by the words of the prophet:

> *"Do not fear, for you will not be ashamed; neither be disgraced, for you will not be put to shame; for you will forget the shame of your youth, and will not remember the reproach of your widowhood anymore" (Isaiah 54:4).*

My dictionary defines reproach as "a cause or occasion of blame, discredit, or disgrace; discredit, disgrace; the act or action of reproaching or disapproving ('was beyond reproach'); an expression of rebuke or disapproval."[1]

Here's my personal definition. *Reproach is the contempt or disdain of other people, or the shame felt in the presence of others, because of one's condition.*

Sometimes reproach is tangible and obvious, in that it may be expressed through words or facial expressions or some similar mode of communication. Sometimes the reproach is only a silent thought. Sometimes, however, it may be totally imagined. The person experiencing the loss may imagine what others are thinking, even when others aren't thinking it. In some cases, a person can feel reproach even when others are actually thinking the opposite—that is, thinking thoughts of honor and

---

[1] Webster's New Collegiate Dictionary, Springfield, MA: G. & C. Merriam Company, 1980, p. 975.

admiration and respect. So reproach either can be real or imagined. But even if it's only imagined, it's still very real to the person feeling it.

One of the characteristics of reproach is the feeling or perception that we are some bizarre exception to the norm, and that no one else on the globe struggles with such wacky losses or emotions. Even though the Scriptures caution us, "Beloved, do not think it strange concerning the fiery trial which is to try you, as though some strange thing happened to you" (1 Peter 4:12), it can be tempting in times of reproach to feel like we are the strangest case to hit planet earth.

THINGS THAT CAN CAUSE REPROACH

We can feel reproached for many reasons. The following is not an exhaustive list, by any means, but represents some of the more common reasons for feeling reproach from others.

RESTRICTION

Involuntary restriction can come in many forms to our lives—physically, emotionally, financially, relationally, etc. When it does, it is often attended by reproach.

For example, when Paul was imprisoned, he recognized that shame naturally wants to visit the prisoner. The shame whispers, "If you were in the right place with God, you wouldn't be sitting here right now, shackled by chains and confined behind bars. You are an embarrassment to the cause of Christ." This is why Paul wrote to Timothy, "Therefore do not be ashamed of the testimony of our Lord, nor of me His prisoner" (2 Timothy 1:8). In speaking of his imprisonment, Paul further said, "For this reason I also suffer these things; nevertheless I am not ashamed, for I know whom I have believed" (2 Timothy 1:12). Paul's knowledge of the person and purposes of Christ empowered him to overcome the assaults of shame.

Paul went on to commend Onesiphorus, because "he often refreshed me, and was not ashamed of my chain" (2 Timothy 1:16). Others had blatantly derided Paul for being in prison (Philippians 1:16), but Onesiphorus did not allow their reproaches to deter him from ministering to God's prisoner.

Are you presently restricted against your will? If so, the reproach you feel is a common experience.

AN INCOMPLETE SPIRITUAL JOURNEY

When God launches you on a unique journey in Him, the pathway can be attended by reproach. The reproach is lifted when others can readily see the final product, but in the interim while you're still in process, shame can hang over your head. For example, Job said, "'I am one mocked by his friends, who called on God, and He answered him, the just and blameless who is ridiculed'" (Job 12:4). Job was saying, "I asked God for something. Then, when He answered my prayer and launched me on a spiritual journey, my friends looked at the incompleteness of where I was at and mocked me for it."

When you're in process, you just want to hang a sign around your neck, "Under Construction." You know that others are also in a process of maturing in God, and yet when you look at their lives, they look so "together." Next to them, you feel like a train wreck.

In discussing this dynamic David wrote, "The reproaches

of those who reproach You have fallen on me" (Psalm 69:9). He was saying, "Others are reproaching me for the spiritual journey I'm on because my life is not a neat package right now. But in reality, Lord, they're reproaching You, because You're the One who called me to this pathway. They're reproaching the means You've chosen to work in my life. So it's really You they're reproaching. But I'm taking the heat for it."

David further added, "For they persecute the ones You have struck, and talk of the grief of those You have wounded" (Psalm 69:26). David was saying, "Lord, I have been struck and wounded by You, my Friend—you have wounded me in faithfulness that I might be trained spiritually in the journey—but others look at my wounds and reproach me for them."

It is frighteningly easy to reproach God for how He chooses to work in a saint's life. We're often not aware that when we make inner heart judgments concerning how someone is walking out his or her journey in God, we in fact are reproaching God Himself. I learned this one the hard way. The Lord has personally rebuked me for the way I used to silently reproach other believers when I saw them walking through difficult circumstances. After the Lord apprehended my life and wounded me, He showed me how I had operated in a judgmental spirit. Now I tremble much more before my Lord, and I guard my heart lest I should carelessly reproach Him for the manner in which He is fashioning one of His vessels.

BARRENNESS

Psalm 127:3 says, "Behold, children are a heritage from the LORD, the fruit of the womb is a reward." In the

Hebrew culture, since children were seen as a direct reward from God, the absence of children was viewed as
a curse from God. So whenever a woman was barren in
Bible times, she unavoidably suffered great reproach.

If a barren woman would eventually give birth to a
child, years of reproach would be lifted from her shoulders. So when Rachel finally gave birth to Joseph, she said,
"'God has taken away my reproach'" (Genesis 30:23). Elizabeth spoke similarly when, after a lifetime of barrenness,
she finally gave birth to John the Baptist: "'Thus the Lord
has dealt with me, in the days when He looked on me,
to take away my reproach among people'" (Luke 1:25).
Oh what a glorious thing, when God takes away your reproach!

One of the most emotion-packed songs in the entire
Bible is the one Hannah sang to the Lord after He had
turned her barrenness into fruitfulness and given her a
son, Samuel (1 Samuel 2:1-10). When we see her tears of
throbbing sorrow, and then behold the exhilaration of her
jubilant song, we cannot help but be gripped by the intensity and anguish of the reproach that barrenness brings.

God uses the reproach of barrenness in a powerful
way to prepare His handmaidens for service. Let me explain. In the three great transitions of redemptive history,
in each instance God birthed His purposes by making a
woman barren. The first transition was when God went
from handling all nations equally, to calling out a special
nation for Himself. How would He navigate this transition? He made a woman barren—Sarah. Her reproach was
unbearable, but eventually the Lord lifted her reproach
and gave her a son of Promise, Isaac, through whom the
new nation would be born.

In the second instance, God wanted to transition His

covenant people from the era of the judges to the era of the kings. How would He help His people make this transition? He made a woman barren. Hannah's barrenness caused her to offer the dangerous prayer that enabled her to give birth to Samuel, the mighty prophet who administrated that great transition by anointing both Saul and David.

But the greatest transition of all yet needed to happen, for God had to move His people from the Old Covenant paradigm to the New Covenant. How would He pull this one off? By making a woman barren. Elizabeth felt untold reproach from her barrenness, but God turned it into great Kingdom fruitfulness by giving her a son in her old age, John the Baptist. It was John, the son of a once-barren woman, who prepared the people for their Messiah.

In each instance, the reproach of barrenness was emotionally overwhelming. But it paved the way for God to manifest restoration and restitution.

UNFULFILLED PROMISES

When you are holding a Promise from God but are not yet inhabiting that Promise, chances are that reproach is troubling your soul. You can probably identify with Psalm 42:10, "As with a breaking of my bones, my enemies reproach me, while they say to me all day long, 'Where is your God?'" Reproach is something you feel all the way to the bone. The adversary adds his taunts, "You say your God loves you, but where is He, now that you need Him? Where is His Promise? Don't you realize that you've been duped?"

When Promise is unfulfilled and you're waiting on God, not only are you battling with reproach, you are also fighting for a sense of personal identity. Identity comes with Promise fulfilled. To substantiate that statement scripturally, let's look at the children of Israel at the time when they finally made it into the Promised Land.

After miraculously crossing the Jordan and entering Canaan, one of the first things God wanted to do with His people was lift their reproach and establish them in their true identity. Their years of slavery and wilderness wanderings made them feel like a band of homeless slaves, but God wanted them established in their identity as the covenant people of God. The Lord addressed these two issues of reproach and identity at Gilgal, the place where He renewed the covenant of circumcision. None of the males born during the wilderness years had been circumcised, so an extensive rite was observed at Gilgal in which all the males were circumcised.

> *Then the LORD said to Joshua, "This day I have rolled away the reproach of Egypt from you." Therefore the name of the place is called Gilgal to this day (Joshua 5:9).*

"The reproach of Egypt" was not the contempt of the Egyptians for the Israelites, but the disdain of Israel's neighbors who regarded them as a band of misplaced Egyptian slaves. Israel had just endured 430 years of slavery and 40 years in the wilderness, so she had 470 years without a national identity. She had no autonomy, no land, no king, and no wealth; little wonder she felt the ridicule of the nations. But upon entering the Promised Land, all this would change. Through circumcision, God declared that their reproach was rolled away from them, and their identity as God's covenant people was fully established.

Circumcision was a rite of identity. "You're Mine. You're in covenant with Me."

Reproach and identity are intertwined. Whenever your identity is undermined, you feel reproach. When God fulfills the Promise you carry, He will both lift the reproach from your life and establish the confidence of your identity as an heir of God. Hallelujah!

POWERLESSNESS

We live in an hour when there is a huge gap between the Gospel we preach and the level of our experience in the Kingdom. We preach a Gospel of power, of healing, of miracles, of signs and wonders, of the resurrection power of Jesus Christ; but what we actually experience falls woefully short of the fullness we proclaim. The demonized come to our meetings and leave with their demons; the handicapped come in their wheelchairs and leave in their wheelchairs; they come to the meeting blind and leave blind; they come deaf and leave deaf. The lack of power in the church, at least in America, has us living under a great shroud of reproach.

Whenever your identity is undermined, you feel reproach.

Our spiritual impotence taunts and ridicules us, much like Goliath who defied the armies of Israel. Just as the entire army shivered under Goliath's diatribe, so today's church quivers before an uncircumcised foe we seem powerless to overcome.

The Lord had in mind the church's impotence when He said, "'I will gather those who sorrow over the appointed assembly, who are among you, to whom its reproach is a burden'" (Zephaniah 3:18). God said He will gather together the intercessors who are burdened by the reproach that hangs over the appointed assembly. I, for one, feel keenly the reproach over our assemblies. We say that Christ is present in our midst, but the manifestations of power that attended His earthly ministry are almost absent from our congregations. The only fitting response is to allow the reproach of our powerlessness to catapult us into unrelenting prayer that we might contend for the fullness of the Kingdom in this generation.

APOSTOLIC LIFESTYLES

There is a reproach that naturally attends the abandoned lifestyles that characterize true apostles. This dynamic was at work in Paul's ministry, and in his writings he gave us a window to this aspect of his world.

> *For I think that God has displayed us, the apostles, last, as men condemned to death; for we have been made a spectacle to the world, both to angels and to men (1 Corinthians 4:9).*

Paul was saying that because of the rigors his apostolic calling placed on his life, he felt like a gazing stock to men. He was like a naked flagpole perched atop a hill, stationed for the entire world to gape at. When people looked at the anomalies and hardships of his life, they scratched their heads and said things like, "What, in heaven's name, is God doing with Paul?"

But it didn't stop there. Paul said that *even the angels* were looking at his life, scratching their heads and saying, "What, in heaven's name, is God doing with Paul?" It's one thing when people are puzzled by your life; it's another thing when angels can't figure you out. Apostles live under such reproach that even the angels are mystified by their journey.

One of the things that Paul felt reproach over was the thorn he carried in his flesh (see 2 Corinthians 12). I believe he was referring to that thorn when he wrote, "You know that because of physical infirmity I preached the gospel to you at the first. And my trial which was in my flesh you did not despise or reject, but you received me as an angel of God, even as Christ Jesus" (Galatians 4:13-14). It could have been tempting for the believers to despise Paul because the great man of faith had a physical infirmity he couldn't overcome. The Galatian believers were commended for looking past the obvious and seeing God's hand in Paul's weakness. We are coming into a day when God's apostles will once again bear in their flesh a thorn that has been divinely allowed, for a season, for strategic Kingdom purpose.

It's one thing when people are puzzled by your life; it's another thing when angels can't figure you out.

When some ministries teach about the restoration of apostles in the church today, they speak in such a way that everyone wants to be one. But the New Testament paradigm of apostolic ministry involved reproach and dishonor. Endtime apostles will once again be spectacles in their generation, living under the reproach of a lifestyle that draws criticism and questions from many observers.

HOW SHOULD WE RESPOND TO REPROACH?

When you first experience reproach, it usually impacts you more forcefully that you would have anticipated. Shame leaves the soul stinging. Initially, you're taken aback because it often comes from sources you didn't expect, in times and ways you didn't expect. The pain of reproach often derives its power from the fact that you warmly esteem those who are reproaching you. Little wonder the psalmist wrote, "Turn away my reproach which I dread" (Psalm 119:39). It's normative, in the initial stages, to *dread* it and seek any avenue of reprieve.

After a while, however, you begin to realize that the reproach is an essential part of the refining process, designed by God for your maturity. Slowly you begin to accept it. Jeremiah's words become helpful—words penned in the aftermath of the dreadful fall of the city of Jerusalem:

> *Let him sit alone and keep silent, because God has laid it on him; let him put his mouth in the dust—there may yet be hope. Let him give his cheek to the one who strikes him, and be full of reproach (Lamentations 3:28-30).*

This is good advice from Jeremiah. Prostrate yourself, place your mouth in the dust, and take to yourself the full weight of the reproach. Accept the cup of trembling the Master has placed in your hand; *drink it* to the bottom. Drain the dregs. Eat dust.

Then, having drunk deeply, *despise* the reproach. Disdain the disdain, just as Jesus did.

> *...looking unto Jesus, the author and finisher of our faith, who for the joy that was set before Him endured the cross, despising the shame, and has sat down at the right hand of the throne of God (Hebrews 12:2).*

On the cross, Jesus keenly felt the reproach of men (Psalm 22:6). But He despised the shame of people's opinions while He hung on the cross. The only way He could do that was by having total disregard for all opinions but one—the opinion of God.

Jesus knew that, if they had understanding, they would have gazed upon Him with wonder and admiration. They reproached Him because they had no idea what a great warfare He was fighting on their behalf. Similarly, people reproach you because they don't understand the nature of your journey in God. They don't realize you're contending for Kingdom realities that will redound to their benefit.

So be unmoved and unfazed by their reproach. Press forward in grace, suffer in the will of God, engage the enemy in warfare, set your love upon your Father, despise the reproaches of men, and lay hold of the very thing for which Christ laid hold of you.

And finally, *take pleasure* in the reproach. I've got Paul's wording in mind.

> *Therefore I take pleasure in infirmities, in reproaches, in needs, in persecutions, in distresses, for Christ's sake. For when I am weak, then I am strong (2 Corinthians 12:10).*

How could Paul take pleasure in reproaches and infirmities? That is one of the great questions of the Kingdom, and one that I have not yet adequately uncovered. It's easy to assent to the verse—until you actually experience infirmities and reproaches. Once they hit, you discover it's much more challenging to take pleasure in them than you thought. I'm still after Paul's secret of taking pleasure in reproaches and needs. For me it is still a pursuit, not an attainment. Therefore, my insight here is limited.

It seems that Moses found the same grace that Paul found.

> *By faith Moses, when he became of age, re-*
> *fused to be called the son of Pharaoh's daugh-*
> *ter, choosing rather to suffer affliction with the*
> *people of God than to enjoy the passing plea-*
> *sures of sin, esteeming the reproach of Christ*
> *greater riches than the treasures in Egypt; for he*
> *looked to the reward (Hebrews 11:24-26).*

This passage says that Moses esteemed the reproach of Christ "greater riches than the treasures in Egypt." He viewed the reproach as "riches."

The Israelites were living in poverty, oppression, and abuse, and yet in faith Moses chose to associate with them rather than with the wealthy courtiers of Pharaoh's opulent palace. And when he felt the reproach of his Egyptian peers, he considered their reproach to be "riches." Moses, how can you view reproach as riches? I am straining to attain this grace.

Additionally, let's go to another verse in Hebrews.

> *...partly while you were made a spectacle both*
> *by reproaches and tribulations, and partly while*
> *you became companions of those who were so*
> *treated (Hebrews 10:33).*

According to this verse, there's two ways to view yourself when suffering reproach and tribulation. You can see yourself as a spectacle, or you can see yourself as a companion—a companion, that is, of the greatest saints who ever lived. You're a companion of the mightiest spiritual giants of all time who also felt the sting of reproach and the distress of tribulation. You can dwell upon the fact that you feel like a naked flagpole on a hill, a spectacle before the gaping multitudes; or you can dwell upon the fact that you are in the company of a great cloud of holy witnesses who have suffered the reproach of men but have endured and gained the prize of their upward calling in Christ.

So I'm making a decision right now. Instead of seeing myself as a spectacle who is hung out to dry before the world, I am going to see myself as a companion of the greatest men and women who ever lived—saints who persevered in prayer and holiness until they obtained their reward. Experiencing this reproach has placed me in the company of the noblest people of all time. Therefore, I will take pleasure in this reproach!

Reproach?

I dread it.

I drink it.

I despise it.

I delight in it.

SHAMED, BUT NOT ASHAMED

I want to distinguish between "shame" and "being ashamed." Look carefully how those terms appear in this passage.

Let not those who wait for You, O Lord GOD of hosts, be ashamed because of me; let not those who seek You be confounded because of me, O God of Israel. Because for Your sake I have borne reproach; shame has covered my face (Psalm 69:6-7).

We see here that David experienced shame, and yet he prayed that none who wait on the Lord might be ashamed. It's one thing to experience shame; it's another altogether to be ashamed. Let me explain.

Shame and reproach refer to the temporary feelings of scorn and derision you experience when you are in a place of distress and are waiting upon God for Him to finish your story. "Ashamed" has to do with the final verdict. "Ashamed" is the final sentence upon a race that was run in vain. When the last chapter has finally been written, some will be ashamed of how their life ends.

But not you. You will never be ashamed. You may have endured shame and reproach in this life, but that reproach is merely the temporary appraisal of people as they have sought to evaluate your life. What really counts is the final verdict. At the end of the race, what will the Judge say?

It's appropriate to print Paul's affirmation here:

For I know that this will turn out for my deliverance through your prayer and the supply of the Spirit of Jesus Christ, according to my earnest expectation and hope that in nothing I shall be ashamed, but with all boldness, as always, so now also Christ will be magnified in my body, whether by life or by death (Philippians 1:19-20).

Paul was bold, even when facing the shame of imprisonment, for he was confident that in the end he would not be ashamed. He would not allow shame to control his destiny because he knew it was not the closing statement on his life. When the last sentence was finally written, the shame was lifted from Paul's life and he was fully vindicated by the Holy Spirit. He now shares the honor of being considered by many the quintessential example of an endtime apostle.

I want to close this chapter by mentioning a verse that is so fierce in its intensity that it literally rumbles through the corridors of history, roaring with resounding authority, underscored by the rolling thunder of heaven's symphonic timpani.

"For they shall not be ashamed who wait for Me"
(Isaiah 49:23).

O the sheer force of the statement! It could not strike with greater impact. Those who wait for God shall not be ashamed! They may be shamed by reproach, but that shame will not be their final verdict. In the end, the righteousness of their journey will be proven before heaven and earth. The wisdom of their choices will be vindicated. They waited for God to get justice for them from their adversary, and in the end they were not ashamed. God bore long with them, but then He visited them with the "speedily of God," turned their reproach to honor, and avenged them of their adversary.

Moses was not ashamed. David was not ashamed. Jeremiah was not ashamed. Jesus was not ashamed. Paul was not ashamed. Nor will you be ashamed. Lift your eyes to your Judge, offer your unrelenting cry to Him, and wait upon Him to avenge you speedily of your adversary.

You shall not be ashamed!

10

NO OTHER OPTION

One of the striking dynamics in our parable is that the widow had no one else to turn to, except the unjust judge of her city. If she was to get justice, she had no other recourse or alternative. It was the judge or it was nothing. This is such a powerful element in the parable that it deserves further contemplation.

It was her realization that the judge was her only hope that put a certain strident desperation in her voice. When she accosted the judge with her cry, he was able to read between the lines. He discerned that this woman was never going to give up. He realized that, if he didn't respond to her cry, the only thing that would shut her up would be death itself.

The power of her cry derived from the fact that he was her only source of help.

The power of her cry derived from the fact that he was her only source of help—hence her intensity and focus.

There is a similar chutzpah and tenacity that comes

to the payer-life of the saint who makes God his or her only option. When God is your only salvation, you gain the single-mindedness that comes with tunnel vision. Distractions lose their power. You become a person of *one thing*. The all-consuming passion becomes, "I must gain Christ!"

"Unrelenting" by definition signifies a singular focus. The word itself carries the idea of contending in prayer and never looking elsewhere until the answer comes. Unrelenting prayer is prayer that contends "until"—until Promise is fulfilled.

I have observed that we never abandon ourselves fully to unrelenting prayer until we cut the ropes that keep other options dangling. As long as we have an alternative besides God, we eventually end up going with it. God wants to save us, but He doesn't want to be one of several remedies we're experimenting with. He wants to be the solitary Life Preserver to which we cling.

AGE OF OPTIONS

We live in a land of seemingly endless options. Our pursuit of Plan A has a certain laissez-faire air about it because, if it doesn't work out, there's always Plan B. And Plan C. And Plan D. Options have become standard topography in the landscape of our digital, post-modern era.

But it's the glut of options that has diluted the potency of our spiritual pursuit. We lack the focus of the widow who hounded the unjust judge's every step. Rather than camping on God's doorstep, we visit God with our requests, but if He doesn't answer in our time frame, we're off to check out the playing field. When we come to God in prayer, we often have a contingency plan already tucked quietly in the back of our minds. "After all," your adversary suggests, "He didn't answer you last time, so why not be prepared just in case He disappoints once again?"

We live in a day when a supernatural answer from God would be nice—but not incontrovertibly necessary. Is it possible that our "age of options" has eviscerated our faith?

Mike Bickle has said that another word for *temptation* is *options*. The more options we have, the more impotent we become. Options often constitute a distraction from the will of God. America has been called the land of opportunity, and rightfully so. Opportunity accompanies modernization—which means that the closer we draw to Christ's appearing, the more our options will abound. Perhaps this is one reason Jesus asked the question, "Nevertheless, when the Son of Man comes, will He really find faith on the earth?" He knew that in the modernization of the last days there would come option proliferation and with it an explosion of opportunities to abandon faith.

And yet, in this final hour, there are many saints to whom God has given the faith[1] to set aside their options and seek Him as the only source of their deliverance. As I write, this is where I find myself. I am waiting on God to heal me and have chosen to forego all other sources of help—such as another surgery—in order to contend for divine healing. During the first year of this vocal affliction I sought medical help (including surgery). But after a year it became clear that this imprisonment was orchestrated of the Lord—and since the God who put Joseph in prison got him out of prison, I have decided to seek the Lord until He gets me out.

Now, as I share my story, let me make clear that I am

---

[1] Faith is a gift from God, Ephesians 2:8.

not against doctors. Many believers have sensed a divine call to a medical profession. I see it as a noble thing to extend care and compassion to wounded, sick, and distressed sufferers. Nor am I critical of those who seek medical attention. I have consulted doctors in the past and will seek medical attention for future needs if the Lord should so direct. But as regards my vocal infirmity, I hold to my confidence that God purposes to deliver me by His power, and that I am to seek Him passionately and exclusively for His healing power.

Some believers have told me how the Lord specifically directed them to go to a doctor. In some of those instances, their subsequent healing was a compelling testimony to the medical community in that region. In other cases, the Lord has put it in the heart of believers to seek no medical help, but to wait entirely upon the Lord for His healing. *I am writing this chapter especially for those in whom God has placed a resolve to wait upon Him only.*

I found that, when I purposed in my heart to wait upon God alone, I entered a fairly intense level of spiritual warfare. It seemed that my adversary did not want me waiting on God. Options for relief seemed to present themselves in so many ways and with such compelling attractiveness. My soul became a battleground. I seemed to be barraged by voices compelling me to check out my options. And I'm not the only one who has experienced this. Any saint who resolves to make God his or her only source of deliverance will face the same war.

For those of you currently in that war, I want to share some of the Scriptures that have encouraged and empowered me to maintain my resolve of seeking God only. When other options are readily available and the wait becomes long, it's tempting to cease crying out to God and look, instead, to another source. Understanding the nature of this battleground, I want to be one of the voices who says, "Wait on God alone." I hope that what I share now may help you to never lose heart, but to cry out to your Judge until He gets justice for you from your adversary.

WAITING ON GOD

I have found great consolation in the Scriptures that speak of waiting on God alone.

Truly my soul silently waits for God; from Him comes my salvation. He only is my rock and my salvation; He is my defense; I shall not be greatly moved...My soul, wait silently for God alone, for my expectation is from Him. He only is my rock and my salvation; He is my defense; I shall not be moved. In God is my salvation and my glory; the rock of my strength, and my refuge, is in God. Trust in Him at all times, you people; pour out your heart before Him; God is a refuge for us. Selah (Psalm 62:1-2, 5-8).

The witness of Scripture is very consistent along this line. God really does want to be our God. He really does want us looking to Him alone for salvation. He delights to demonstrate His supernatural power.

I know only one way to wait on God: To wait on Him alone. No Plan B. To wait on Him until. To wait on Him until He answers. No contingencies. Anything short of that is not waiting.

I know only one way to wait on God: To wait on Him alone. No Plan B.

SAUL WOULDN'T WAIT

Sometimes I learn best either by doing it wrong or watching someone else do it wrong. That's why I find it helpful to look at King Saul, a man who failed to wait upon God and paid a steep price for it. The cost, in fact, was his very life. He died as a direct consequence of turning to a medium instead of waiting on the Lord for spiritual counsel. Notice what the Holy Spirit said about his death.

> *So Saul died for his unfaithfulness which he had committed against the LORD, because he did not keep the word of the LORD, and also because he consulted a medium for guidance. But he did not inquire of the LORD; therefore He killed him, and turned the kingdom over to David the son of Jesse (1 Chronicles 10:13-14).*

These verses tell us that Saul was taken out for three main sins: He was unfaithful against the Lord; he did not obey the word of the LORD to totally destroy the Amalekites[2]; and he inquired of a medium instead of the LORD. Here's the passage that describes the time Saul sought the help of a medium:

> *When Saul saw the army of the Philistines, he was afraid, and his heart trembled greatly. And when Saul inquired of the LORD, the LORD did not answer him, either by dreams or by Urim or by the prophets. Then Saul said to his servants,*

---

[2] 1 Samuel 15.

"Find me a woman who is a medium, that I may go to her and inquire of her." And his servants said to him, "In fact, there is a woman who is a medium at En Dor" (1 Samuel 28:5-7).

The nation of Israel was being invaded by the Philistines, who were both more numerous and better equipped than the Israelites. Saul was terrified at the threat they posed. He attempted to consult the Lord, but the Lord wouldn't answer him. Desperate for guidance, Saul asked a medium to bring Samuel back from the dead so he could get sound guidance from Samuel. What Saul *should* have said is, "Lord, I am in desperate circumstances. I need to make an immediate decision, and You're not talking to me. But I'm not moving. I'm staying right here before You, in brokenness and desperation, until You talk to me. The Philistines are coming, and if You don't talk to me they're going to totally overwhelm us, because I'm not doing a thing until You answer me." Had Saul waited on God like this, everything would have been different. But in his desperation for an immediate answer, he turned to a medium, and God killed him for it.

When God doesn't answer you right away, you may be in a test. What will you do when heaven is silent? Wrong answer: Go to Plan B. Right answer: Wait on God.

DAVID WAITED ON GOD

This is one of the primary things that distinguished David from Saul. Saul couldn't wait; but David was a man who had learned to wait on God—until. Look at what he wrote:

I waited patiently for the LORD; and He inclined to me, and heard my cry (Psalm 40:1).

My soul, wait silently for God alone, for my expectation is from Him (Psalm 62:5).

When David said he waited "patiently," it does not mean that he was without angst. Nor does it mean that he was always silent, nor passive, nor docile, nor leisurely, nor compliant. It simply means that he looked to God alone and refused to court any other option. It means that he did not lose heart but lifted his cry without ceasing to his Judge.

Look at David's life, and you'll see what it means to wait patiently. You fill your lungs; bring your vocal cords together; let out your cry of anguish and pain; lift your voice without ceasing to God; find fresh assurance in His Word; breathe in His grace; your soul gently begins to quiet, and you come to a new place of rest; faith is renewed and confidence restored. Then the next day it happens all over again. And the next. In this manner, the soul comes to a new place of resolve every day: "I will wait on God alone." This is what it means to wait patiently.

One of the more fascinating moments in David's journey was the time when two men brought the head of Ishbosheth to David. (Ishbosheth, one of Saul's sons, was David's rival, and because he was still reigning in Israel, it meant that David was reigning over just one tribe of Israel, the tribe of Judah.) When these two men killed Ishbosheth and brought his head to David, they knew they had removed a massive obstacle that hindered David's destiny. With Ishbosheth gone, there would be virtually nothing else to stop the immediate fulfillment of God's

Promise that David would reign over the entire nation. So they expected David to greet them with gratefulness and enthusiasm. But what did David do? He executed them both on the spot (2 Samuel 4:8-12)! David's attitude was basically this: "God has given me a Promise, and God is the One who will fulfill it for me. So don't you try to help God out. I'm not interested in human meddling to try to fulfill God's Word on my behalf. Leave my Promise alone. I don't need man's help. God is the One who will fulfill His Word to me." Those who tried to help David enter His promises paid a steep price for presumptuously inserting themselves into that which was God's business. In the same way, we're not interested in a human solution. God gave the Promise; He will fulfill it. We will wait on Him alone.

David wrote what has become one of the strongest cries of my soul: "Let not those who wait for You, O Lord GOD of hosts, be ashamed because of me" (Psalm 69:6). When I pray that verse to God I say things like, "Lord, I'm waiting on You alone. And there are a whole lot of people watching this thing play out. May it never be, Lord, that they should behold me waiting on You, decide that waiting doesn't work, and be too ashamed themselves to wait on You. May it never be! I want the testimony of my life to empower them to wait on You. May they watch my life and see that it pays to wait on God!"

In Psalm 27, David handed down his best wisdom after testing God in this thing: "Wait on the LORD; be of good courage, and He shall strengthen your heart; wait, I say, on the LORD!" (Psalm 27:14). I hear David saying, "Take it from a guy who has proven the faithfulness of God. I waited patiently on the Lord, and wow, did He ever come through for me! It wasn't in the time frame I was looking for. The wait was outside my comfort zones. But still I waited. And when God finally came through for me, it was beyond all that I could ask or imagine. So I'm telling you: Don't take matters into your own hands. Wait on the Lord!"

Let me mention one more passage in David that really seals my resolve to seek the Lord only:

> *I will cry out to God Most High, to God who performs all things for me. He shall send from heaven and save me...My heart is steadfast, O God, my heart is steadfast; I will sing and give praise (Psalm 57:2,7).*

When David said his heart was steadfast, he had several things in mind.[3] But I like to think that his heart was steadfast, above all, in the confidence that God would send from heaven and save him. He was convinced—more than that—he held a firm conviction that God would save him from his enemies. His heart was fixated upon that certainty. I hear David saying, "I'm in such a mess that there's no way I will ever get out based upon my own ingenuity or power. But my God has given me a Promise. Therefore, I am absolutely persuaded that He will reach from heaven above, stretch down to this earth, and deliver me by His supernatural power. You just watch. It's going to happen! I'm more convinced than ever. My eyes are on God alone, and I will never be moved from this confidence. He alone is my Deliverer, and He shall deliver me."

When I behold David's resolve to wait for God to send from heaven, I am encouraged to do likewise.

---

[3] To see this, read Psalm 57 in its entirety.

My commitment to unrelenting prayer is bolstered. I am emboldened with confidence to declare, "God performs all things for me. He will send from heaven and save me." Just watch. It's going to happen. "I will sing and give praise."

Make Psalm 57 your own. Set your heart steadfastly to wait on God. May your heart be steadfast in crying to God until He avenges you of your adversary!

JACOB WAITED ON GOD

When my wait seems interminable and I am tempted to lose heart in prayer, I find great encouragement in the example of Jacob. Jacob was a man who waited on God for His salvation, and even though he waited many years he eventually saw the day when God sent from heaven and saved him.

Jacob's entire life was devoted to seeking God (even though he didn't always do it right). He was such a passionate pursuer of heaven that the Scriptures indicate this was the defining characteristic of his life (Psalm 24:6). So if you are a God-seeker, you have the heart of Jacob. Jacob is the believer who seeks God only and waits upon Him to fulfill His Word. Lord, give me the heart of Jacob. I want to wait on You like he did because I want to touch what he touched.

One of the fascinating characteristics of Jacob's story is that most of his life was spent waiting. Little bursts of divine activity were separated by long expanses of virtual inactivity. Jacob himself attested to this when he said, "'I have waited for your salvation, O LORD!'" (Genesis 49:18). It's very easy to gloss right over this brief statement from Jacob, but it actually summarizes Jacob's life message. His was a life of waiting.

Consider the large spans of inactivity in Jacob's life:

- Up to age 75, we have one recorded activity in Jacob's life, the time when Esau sold him the birthright for a bowl of stew. Other than that, his story starts with 75 years of waiting.

- At age 75, he tricks his father into blessing him, and then flees from his brother to Haran. He has a flurry of divine activity at this point in his journey, for he sees a ladder with angels on it, and God speaks directly to him of His sovereign plans and assurances.

- During the next 20 years of life in Haran, there is a fair level of activity in his life as he marries two sisters and fathers eleven sons. But there is no gripping spiritual activity during those 20 years. The next big event happens when he returns to Canaan at age 95. He has a life-altering encounter with God at Peniel, and receives both his new name and his limp.

- Then we have 13 years of silent waiting, until Jacob is 108, at which time Joseph is sold into slavery.

- Then there's 22 additional years of silent waiting in Jacob's life, during which time Joseph is in Egypt. We hear nothing about Jacob during these 22 long years.

- It's not until Jacob is 130 that we meet up with him again, at which time he is severely distressed by a famine and the loss of his sons Simeon and

Benjamin. It is here, however, that all of Jacob's fortunes turn. He is reunited not only with Simeon and Benjamin, but also with Joseph. Furthermore, his family is amply provided for in Goshen throughout the remaining years of the famine. So for the last 17 years of his life, until his death at age 147, Jacob inherits the fruit of living a life waiting upon God.

Jacob's life was comprised mostly of waiting on God. But because he refused to break covenant with his God and because he refused to brook any other sources of salvation, God eventually came to him in his sunset years and lavished upon him the fullness of His provision and promises.

More than 20 Bible verses describe God as "the God of Jacob" (for example, see Psalm 46:7,11). In other words, God continues to deal with us today the same way He did with Jacob. This encourages me when I, like Jacob, endure many years of unfulfilled promises. I know that the God of Jacob never changes! He who honored Jacob will also honor me because I too am a Jacob who seeks His face.

Jacob's life has been given to us, according to Psalm 46, as a prophetic picture of the kind of battle the saints will face at the end of the age.[4] In the last days nations will rage and kingdoms will be moved. Then the Lord will utter His voice, and the earth will literally melt (Psalm 46:6; 2 Peter 3:10). God will demonstrate Himself as the refuge

---

[4] Psalm 46 is an eschatological psalm, pointing to the upheaval that will happen at the end of the Gospel age, and the desolations that Jesus will make in the earth when He returns to establish His millennial rule. In the context of speaking of this endtime drama, Psalm 46 points to Jacob twice—in verses 7 and 11. The inference to be drawn is that Jacob's story is intended to comfort and empower the saints at the end of the age.

of His people (Psalm 46:7; Zechariah 14:3). And then the saints will "behold the works of the LORD, who has made desolations in the earth" (Psalm 46:8), for the desolations of Revelation 16 through 19 will display the mighty right hand of our God.

As it was for Jacob at age 130, so will it be for the elect at the end of the age. Because of the famine, Jacob felt like heaven was against him (Genesis 42:36); similarly, the saints will wonder at times if heaven is against them because of the intensity of their distresses. Jacob was opposed by the main political figure of his day, the powerful leader in Egypt who was second only to Pharaoh; similarly, the saints will have the most powerful man on the planet against them (the antichrist, Revelation 13:1-8). Jacob was betrayed by his sons when they lied about Joseph's enslavement; similarly, betrayal from family members will be rampant in the last days (Mark 13:12). As it was with Jacob, the forces pitted against the saints will be so horribly bizarre as to seem surreal. The question will be: Will the elect of God wait on Him alone and cry out to Him night and day? Or will they waiver in faith, lose heart, and stop contending for Promise? In that day, blessed are those who, like Jacob, will wait for the salvation of God. The God of Jacob will be their refuge and their God!

WHAT IS A FALSE GOD?

God called Isaiah to his prophetic ministry at a time when the nation was plagued with idolatry. Many had lost faith in Jehovah's ability to provide for them and had turned to the gods of their neighbors. In response, Isaiah repeatedly urged the people to turn from all other sources of deliverance to the Lord alone.

Isaiah was openly sarcastic about the people's idolatrous penchant. With ridicule, he poked at the practice of chopping a piece of wood in two, using one part to stoke a fire for warmth and cooking, and then carving a god out of the remainder. Here's what the man carving the image does, according to Isaiah: "He falls down before it and worships it, prays to it and says, 'Deliver me, for you are my god!'" (Isaiah 44:17).

This verse says that a false god was worshiped because the idolater believed the block of wood could deliver him. Herein we find a definition for what constitutes a false god. According to Isaiah 44:17, *a god is anything to which we ascribe the power to deliver us.*

In today's western world, we don't always think of ourselves as having false gods because we no longer carve images out of blocks of wood. But by looking at the above definition of a false god, we suddenly see that we are a culture that is *filled* with false gods. There are so many things to which we Americans ascribe the power to deliver us. We don't have gods of carved wood today; instead, we look for deliverance from sources such as money, Social Security, retirement accounts, health insurance, the medical industry, drugs, alcohol, food, sex, creature comforts, etc. Most of these things are not wrong in their rightful place, and some can even be a means of divine provision, but all have the potential to gain misplaced emphasis in our souls.

Watch TV commercials, and you will see many of the American gods on display. They are constantly vying for our attention: "Buy me; I will relieve you." "Come to me; I will help you." "Our product will make you happy and content." "Our dating service is the answer to your loneliness." We may no longer carve gods out of wood, but we have more gods today than ever.

If I am to walk with the Lord in an idolatrous age such as ours, I must have a guard around my heart. Isaiah 44:17 has helped me to recognize what constitutes a false god, which in turn helps me to keep my eyes on the Lord. I want a heart that is pure before God. I don't want to look to another source for deliverance when God wants to be my deliverance.

Lord, help me to tremble before You, and to ever make You my only God. To You alone I ascribe the power to deliver me.

DOVE'S EYES

In the Song of Solomon the Lord calls us His dove. More than once He has said that we have "dove's eyes" (Song of Solomon 1:15; 4:1). The significance of what it means to have dove's eyes was reinforced to me once, many years ago. At the time, I was driving down the highway at about 50 miles per hour, and in the distance I could see a pair of turtledoves slowly waddling out onto the highway. As I approached them I thought to myself, "You better move. I don't swerve for birds or animals." (I've heard of too many horror stories in which a driver swerved to avoid an animal or bird, and as a result a human being was hurt or killed. So I've adopted a no-swerve driving policy.) But they just kept on meandering out onto the road. By the time they saw me, it was too late. BAM! I hit them both at 50 mph. Looking in my rearview mirror, I saw a plume of feathers billowing into the air behind me. As I continued down the road, I thought to myself, "Stupid birds. Should have moved."

It was later that I learned: *Turtledoves have no periph-*

eral vision. The lovebirds didn't even see me coming!

When Jesus tells us we have dove's eyes, He is saying, "You have eyes for Me only. I am all that you see. Your head is not turned to other saviors or redeemers. I am your only salvation."

So my lovesick eyes are focused constantly upon the One I adore. I have no alternatives. He alone is my Savior and my Deliverer. As His dove, I look to Him only and wait upon Him until He rises up to answer my cry and get justice for me from my adversary. From this single-hearted focus I shall not be moved. Where else shall I go? He alone has authority over my adversary.

RELIEF OR SALVATION?

Let's return to the widow of our Luke 18 parable. Had she been interested in being comforted in the midst of her pain, she could have received comfort from a friend. If she were wanting empathy or sympathy, she could have turned to a neighbor. If she were seeking help with food or clothing, she could have sought out a benevolent institution. Had she been satisfied with a handout, she could have begged on the street. If a little relief would have sufficed, perhaps she could have asked the police for a temporary restraining order against her adversary. But she didn't want any of those things. She raised her eyes to the highest objective possible: *justice.* But in setting her sights on so lofty a prize, she realized she had but one place to get such a grand attainment—the judge. If it was justice she wanted, he was her only option. The point for us is this: *The grandeur of the quest usually determines the number of options at your disposal.* The lower your gaze, the more abundant your alternatives. Set your sights high enough, however, and you'll probably find yourself with only one option—God.

I have been confronted with an important question: Do I simply want relief, or do I want God's salvation? If I want relief, then there are many alternatives at my disposal. But if I want to see the mighty salvation of my God, then I have but one option. I can do nothing but wait upon Him. He alone can avenge me with the justice of His salvation.

> *Set your sights high enough, however, and you'll probably find yourself with only one option—God.*

"'Nor is there salvation in any other, for there is no other name under heaven given among men by which we must be saved'" (Acts 4:12). There is no source of salvation among men. Men can help you; they can support you; they can encourage you; they can counsel you; and they can relieve you (although sometimes it can backfire, and you can end up worse than before you solicited their help). But they can't save you.

There is only One who can save, because salvation is a mighty thing. When God saves, it is so thorough and glorious that it is called in Scripture "so great a salvation" (Hebrews 2:3). His salvation reaches to the emotions, the heart, the soul, the mind, the body, the house, the possessions, the family, the neighborhood, the world, the sky—it reaches into eternity. His salvation not only helps, it transforms; it renews; it heals; it restores; it vindicates; it rewards; it makes all things new. So I've decided, I don't simply want relief anymore. I want salvation. I will lift my cry, therefore, to the only One who can save me, and will never relent until I see His glorious salvation here and now in the land of the living.

11

RESTITUTION FOR NAOMI

In Jesus' parable of the persistent widow, the widow is not named, nor do we know the nature of the injustice that her adversary inflicted upon her. That's because Jesus was telling a parable, not a story. But if you want to find an actual biblical story that embodies the message of the parable, the best example would doubtless be the story that is found in the book of Ruth. It is there that the parable of the widow takes on names, faces, places, and historic events.

In this chapter, therefore, I simply want to tell the story—a story about a woman in the Bible named Naomi, and her daughter-in-law, Ruth. I am recounting their story, not only because it is one of the most heartwarming stories in the entire Bible, but also because it illustrates the great principles of this book. Even though God bore long with their cries, there came a glorious moment when they entered into the speedily of God. And when they did, justice brought to them both restoration and restitution. Sit back and enjoy the retelling of this sublime story. As you do, may this reminder of Naomi's saga strengthen your resolve in prayer and renew your confidence in the certainty of God's salvation in your own life.

Naomi and her husband, Elimelech, were a godly couple who lived in Bethlehem together with their two boys, Mahlon and Chilion. Tragedy struck in the form of a famine, however, and Elimelech was forced to leave his beloved homestead and relocate his family to the land of Moab for a period of time, simply to survive.

After living in Moab for a while, tragedy struck again, and Elimelech's life was taken. Naomi was crushed. Left as a single mom, she struggled to raise her boys by herself, and finally managed to marry them off to a couple Moabite girls. However, tragedy struck yet again, and God took the lives of Naomi's two sons. The loss was utterly devastating to Naomi. She had lost all her men, any hope of perpetuating the family name, and all hope of financial security in her elderly years. Now she was left with just two Moabite daughters-in-law. Hit with compound losses, Naomi's soul was entirely entombed in grief and heartache.

Not long afterward, word drifted over to Moab that God had heard the prayers for the land of Israel and had lifted the famine. There was once again bread in Bethlehem (the name Bethlehem means "house of bread"). After living in Moab for ten long years, Naomi packed up her meager belongings and started for home.

Her daughters-in-law, Orpah and Ruth, said, "We're coming with you, Mom." But Naomi replied, "Why would you come with me? It's not as though I have any other sons that could grow up and become your husbands in the course of time. Return, go back to your mothers' houses. May the Lord return to you the kindness you have shown me, and give you Moabite husbands with whom you can be fruitful." So she kissed them both good-bye, and the three of them wept aloud in each other's embrace.

Orpah and Ruth tried to remonstrate, but Naomi said, "My heart is very sorrowful for your sakes that the hand of the Lord has gone out against me. I cannot provide husbands for you. Turn back; why would you go with me?"

So after much weeping, Orpah finally kissed Naomi good-bye and returned to her family. Ruth, however, would not be dissuaded but clung to Naomi. Naomi said, "Orpah has returned; Ruth, go with her!" But Ruth responded with words that have been memorialized for showing not only her genuine affection for Naomi but also her genuine faith in the God of Israel. She said,

> *"Entreat me not to leave you, or to turn back from following after you; for wherever you go, I will go; and wherever you lodge, I will lodge; your people shall be my people, and your God, my God. Where you die, I will die, and there will I be buried. The LORD do so to me, and more also, if anything but death parts you and me" (Ruth 1:16-17).*

Seeing such devotion, Naomi yielded to Ruth's fervor and allowed Ruth to accompany her back to Israel. When the two arrived in Bethlehem, the entire village was abuzz with the news. "Naomi has returned!" the women chattered.

Naomi replied to the women, "Don't call me Naomi. Call me Mara." She said this because the name Naomi meant "Pleasant," whereas the name Mara meant "Bitter." "The Almighty has dealt very bitterly with me," Naomi explained. "I left full, but am returning home empty. God has testified against me and afflicted me. So don't even call me Naomi." Even though she was back in her hometown, Naomi's heart was still overwhelmed with the pain of her losses. She was like a living representation of the widow in Jesus' parable.

Naomi and Ruth secured a small room to rent, and Ruth took up the occupation of the poorest in the land—the business of gleaning in the fields after the reapers had harvested the crops. By chance she found herself gleaning in the fields of a wealthy man named Boaz. Boaz just happened to be a close relative of Elimelech, Naomi's deceased husband. When Boaz was informed of Ruth's identity, he told her to glean in his fields only. He said, "Stay close to my young women. I've commanded my young men not to touch you. And you may drink from the water they draw for my laborers." Boaz acknowledged the kindness Ruth had shown toward Naomi, saying to her, "May the Lord honor your kindness and repay your work with a full reward, under whose wings you have come for refuge."

Furthermore, Boaz urged her to eat of the bread he supplied his laborers, and he even coached the reapers to purposely allow clumps of grain to fall onto Ruth's path, so that Ruth's gleanings might be greater. In these ways, Ruth was able to bring home enough food for her and Naomi to live.

As time went along, Naomi kept hoping that someone might rise up on their behalf and help them in their poverty. But nothing seemed to come their way. Finally, Naomi rose up in her soul, laid hold of faith, and stepped into action. "Sit down, Ruth," I can suppose her saying, "I've got something to talk to you about."

"Okay, Mama, what's on your mind?"

Naomi began to start talking the language of faith. "Ruth, we have a just claim before God. The law of Moses[1] has a provision in it, that if a man dies without leaving an heir to his inheritance, the next closest relative has a God-ordained duty to marry the widow. If the widow then gives birth to a son, that boy is considered to be the son of the deceased husband, and he becomes the heir of the deceased man's estate and the perpetuator of his name. Ruth, I'm cashing in on my just claim before God. I want God to get justice for me from my adversary. It's time to ask for that which is our rightful due as daughters of Abraham."

"I'm with you, Mama. What is your plan? I'll do whatever you want me to do."

So that night Ruth followed Naomi's orders verbatim. She quietly went down to the threshing floor and waited until Boaz had eaten and drunk and fallen asleep. Then she softly slipped over to his sleeping form, uncovered his feet, and laid down there. Around midnight Boaz was awakened by a noise and realized his feet were cold. But when he went to straighten the blanket, there was a woman at his feet! "Who are you?" he asked in a befuddled way, his mind still trying to come fully awake.

"I am Ruth, your maidservant," came the reply. "Cover me with your garment and be my close relative redeemer." With these simple words Ruth was saying, "Marry me. And give me a son who will be the heir to Elimelech's inheritance. Remove from me these black garments of

---

[1] See Deuteronomy 25:5-10 for this provision in Moses' law. Based on the wording in the King James Version rendering of Ruth 3:9, this provision has been affectionately termed "the law of the kinsman redeemer." The close relative literally became a "redeemer" of the dead man's inheritance that was bereft of a male heir.

widowhood that have covered me in reproach and grief these many months. Clothe me, instead, with the bright garments of matrimony in your household of abundance."

Well, by now Boaz was fully awake! He understood entirely what she was asking of him. His response indicated how much he esteemed Ruth's integrity in the matter. "You are blessed of the Lord, my daughter!" Boaz replied. "You didn't seek for a husband among the men your age; rather, you sought to uphold the dignity of your mother-in-law, even if it meant approaching a man as elderly as myself. This is a great kindness you are showing Naomi, so I am saying, 'Yes,' to you. However, there is a man who is an even closer relative to Elimelech than I, and he has the first right in this instance. If he will perform the duty of redeemer for you, then good; but if not, then I will. Lie here till morning, and in the morning I will tend to the necessary business."

Before anyone could recognize Ruth by morning light, Boaz filled her shawl with barley and sent her home to Naomi. When Ruth told Naomi what had happened, Naomi said, "Sit down and rest, Ruth. There's no gleaning in the field for you today. Relax and wait until you hear the outcome of this, because the man will not defer or be distracted with any other business until he has concluded this matter today. Before the day is out, you will know whether you are to be the wife of Boaz or of the closer relative."

Naomi knew something about the character of Boaz. She knew that once Boaz stepped into action, he would not rest until he had finished the matter. The same quality is true of our divine Boaz, Jesus Christ, our true Redeemer. Once our heavenly Boaz rises up and steps into action on our behalf, He will not rest or desist until He has concluded the matter and brought it to its rightful resolution. In other words, when Jesus arises to act on your behalf, you have now entered the speedily of God. Events will shake down rapidly. Once you know that Jesus has risen to your defense, take your place of rest and watch to see what He will do for you.

Sure enough, Boaz went straight to the city gate, had the closer relative join him, gathered a group of witnesses, and asked if he would buy Elimelech's property and marry Ruth in order to raise up an heir. When the closer relative declined, Boaz fulfilled the proper legal requirements to bring Ruth into his home, and the business was completed on the spot. Before the day was out, Ruth was held in the embrace of Boaz, her husband redeemer.

Ruth had not been able to get pregnant with Mahlon, her first husband; but Boaz was no Mahlon. Boaz had some life in him. So when Boaz and Ruth came together, Ruth became impregnated with a baby boy.

When the boy was born, the women of Bethlehem named him Obed and said, "There is a son born to Naomi," because they recognized that the boy would carry on Naomi's and Mahlon's heritage. Obed was the father of Jesse, who was the father of David, the king of Israel. That's why a Moabite widow—Ruth—is named in the genealogy of Jesus Christ (see Matthew 1:5-6).

There are two widows in this story who, after leaning on God's Word to receive their just claim, were granted justice and entered into both restoration and restitution. I'll mention Ruth first. Not only was she a widow, she was also a foreigner. And even though the law proscribed people of Moab from participating in covenant blessings (Deuteronomy 23:3), because of her faith in God's provision in the law, Ruth's widowhood was turned to joyful marriage and motherhood. *The widow became the bride.* Her story illustrates how God will turn the seeming barrenness of our widowhood into the fruitfulness of the Bride of Christ, when we stand in faith and cry out for justice. Not only was Ruth's widowhood turned to fruitfulness, she also entered through faith into the very bloodline of the Messiah Himself.

Naomi was the second widow who received both restoration and restitution. She staked her claim in the Word and got justice from every adversarial thing that had swept her soul. Through faith, she became the mother—vicariously—of Obed, and hence the great-grandmother of the mighty king of Israel, King David. God turned her reproach to honor and gave her a name that stands in the halls of faith as one of the great names of redemptive history.

The widow became the bride.

Little wonder this story made it into the Bible! Its witness thunders through the centuries and grips our souls with the confidence of God's faithfulness. Our hearts soar again with the certainty that when our heavenly Boaz (Jesus) rises up on our behalf, He will avenge us *speedily*. And when He does, He will not only restore what was lost but will also reverse our reproach and crown us with manifold reparations. When Jesus comes to visit us, may He find this confidence resonating in our hearts!

12

A PRISONER NAMED
SIMON ZHAO

I want to end this book with one final story, this time not from the Bible but from our century. This is the story of a modern-day hero of faith, a Chinese prisoner by the name of Simon Zhao[1]. Simon's life is gripping and powerful, and by the time we're finished I think you'll agree that he experienced not only God's restoration, but also a sevenfold restitution for what the adversary had stolen.

Simon's destiny had its beginnings in the 1920s, in a fledgling vision[2] that would develop and eventually come to be called "The Back to Jerusalem Movement." God ignited a passion in the hearts of a small group of Chinese believers to commence a journey by foot toward Jerusalem, evangelizing in all the territories they traversed.

---

[1] His proper Chinese name was Zhao Haizhen.

[2] Simon was part of a 1940s movement then called the "Northwest Spiritual Movement," so named for its vision to target northwest China and regions beyond.

They sold all possessions and forsook friends, family, and careers in order to spread the Gospel message.

The "Back to Jerusalem" vision matured and developed, forming into a mission to take the Gospel to the regions of Asia that were dominated by the three world religions most resistant to the Gospel: the Hindu world, the Buddhist world, and the Muslim world. Since the Gospel came to China from Jerusalem, they wanted to return the favor and take the Gospel back to Jerusalem.

The vision seems to be clearer and more alive today than ever. Many contemporary Chinese believers carry the hope of deploying 100,000 full-time Chinese evangelists into the harvest, launching them toward Jerusalem, with the mandate of impacting the Hindus and Buddhists and Muslims for Christ. Ultimately, the goal is to meet up in Jerusalem to greet the Lord Jesus when He returns and plants His feet on the Mount of Olives.

Whether China will actually deploy 100,000 full-time evangelists toward Jerusalem has been debated, but even if they don't attain that number, the vision is noble and heartwarming!

In the 1940s there were several small groups that had ownership of this vision to take the Gospel through hostile territory back to Jerusalem. They were compelled by a sense of urgency that the Lord's return was imminent. One of the primary leaders at that time was a man named Simon Zhao. Now we come to his story.

Simon burned with a vision to expend his life taking the Gospel beyond the western borders of China. Joined by his new wife, Simon and his small team departed from Nanjing for the remote northwest area of China called Xinjiang. Times were troubled by civil unrest, and travelers hazarded many perils from robbers, weather, and remote wilderness. Moving slowly, they won many converts to Christ as they proceeded.

Protected and helped by the Lord, the team of roughly 25 members finally made it in 1948 to Kashgar (also called Kashi), one of China's most westerly cities. They stopped in Kashgar, gathered their strength, and prepared to launch westward.

But just as they were about to step over the line, the iron fist of Communism descended on the land and the borders clanged shut. Simon's group said, "But we are Christian missionaries with a call to take the Gospel west." When the Communists heard that they wanted across the border, they flatly decreed, "You're traitors!" And they promptly incarcerated the entire band of evangelists, giving extremely harsh sentences to the five top leaders.

Chinese prisons in the 1940s were not like American prisons today. Basically, they were death camps. Conditions in the coal mine labor camp were horrific: a starvation diet, rancid food, grueling labor 14 hours a day and 7 days a week, sweltering summers and harsh winters, with daily torture. Men would come into the labor camps in their strength and in six months be dead.

Simon's wife miscarried their first baby while in prison and then later died herself. The other four primary leaders died. Whether any of the team survived their shorter prison sentences was not clear in the account I read. But the man with the harshest sentence, Simon Zhao the widower, would not die. In retrospect, he realized God was preserving him supernaturally.

The months turned into years. Five years. Ten years. Fifteen years. Now, I never met Simon Zhao personally, nor have I ever been in a Chinese prison. But I have been in a prison of a different kind—a prison of physical affliction—and I have come to discover that although there are many kinds of prisons, the emotional responses of prisoners are virtually the same, even if the nature of the prisons are different. All prisoners must grapple with feelings of despondency, depression, loneliness, hopelessness, boredom, listlessness, etc. So even though I was not told much about his emotional turmoil in those years, I can promise you this much: Simon's vision of taking the Gospel west was crushed in short order. Prison has a cruel way of annihilating one's sense of purpose and destiny. Simon entered prison in his prime—at age 32—a young man brimming with potential and passion for gathering the harvest. The visionary side of Simon was soon decimated, however, and was replaced with a survival mode. Simon's life-vision became, "Let's see if I can make it one more day."

Nevertheless, Simon never let go of his God. Nor did he forget to pray, "Lord, I will never be able to go to Jerusalem, but I pray you will raise up a new generation of Chinese believers who will complete the vision."

15 years. 20 years. 25 years. Simon almost died more than once but managed to recuperate each time. On the verge of death at one point, he was transferred to another prison where he worked in a chemical factory. But it was hardly an improvement, being exposed daily as he was to toxic gases and chemicals.

He was beaten, tortured, and abused daily, either by the guards or the other prisoners. (The guards devised ways to turn the prisoners on each other, the Muslim prisoners being especially malicious.) And yet there were tokens of the Lord's favor upon his life. For instance, on one occasion the other prisoners locked him out of the barracks in the dead of winter with no outer clothing, taunting him to see if his God would help him. Simon cried out to the Lord and suddenly felt warm all over.The prisoners were astounded to look outside and see steam rising off his body and the snow melting around his feet.

On another occasion, he was beaten so severely that his skull was fractured.While unconscious, the Lord came to him in a vision and said,"My child, I am with you. I shall never leave you or forsake you." Regaining consciousness, he touched the spot where his skull was smashed, and although there was dried blood on the spot, the wound had been miraculously healed.

25 years. 30 years.After 30 years in prison, Simon said they finally stopped torturing him daily.

30 years. 35 years.

Simon had been given a 45-year sentence. After 40 years in prison, he was called one day in 1988 into the warden's office. He stepped gingerly before the warden, apprehensive that his sentence might be extended yet again for some unpredictable reason.To his surprise, the warden said, "The government of the People's Republic of China has decided to be merciful and lenient to you for the crimes you have committed against our nation. I have been authorized to release you five years early.You are free to go."

Dazed, Simon shuffled out of the prison onto the streets of Kashgar, a thin, white-bearded little man. He was about 72 years old, with a body that carried the marks of decades of beatings, torture, and hard work. Since his imprisonment in 1948, China had gone through the Cultural Revolution and had seen so many changes that Simon could hardly recognize his own nation. He hadn't had a solitary visitor in 40 years. Of those who had known him 40 years earlier, most were dead. Of those living, none had any idea of Simon's whereabouts or that he was still alive. He didn't know his nation and he didn't know a single soul. So now what?

He did the only thing he knew to do—he found a small room and prayed. Eventually a believer stumbled onto him, and word leaked out among the Christians in Kashgar, "A brother is here who has just survived 40 years in prison for his faith." They came to him to hear his story, and helped him with food and a Bible.

The news gradually seeped across China, "One of the founding fathers of the Back to Jerusalem Movement has just survived 40 years in the Chinese prison system, and is living in Kashgar." When the news made its way to eastern China, the believers were stunned. Forty years in Chinese prisons?? Unthinkable!

In 1988, the revival among the underground churches in eastern China was perhaps at its zenith. New converts were coming to Christ daily in droves. And nowhere were the flames hotter than in Henan Province. Dubbed by some the "Galilee" of the current Chinese revival, Henan was the epicenter of the underground house church movement in 1988.

When some leaders in Henan learned of Simon's existence, they immediately sent a delegation on the four-day train trek to Kashgar with instructions to bring Simon back at all costs. When they found him, they eagerly asked him about his experiences. He simply and meekly said, "I served 40 years in the Chinese penal system."

They told him, "You must come back with us to Henan."

He said, "No, thank you. I'm fine right here."

They said, "But you must come back with us. You have an important story to tell, and the church needs to hear your story."

He replied, "I have nothing to say. I don't want anyone to know my name. I'm staying here."

They rejoined, "But you don't understand. While you've been in prison, God has ignited a powerful revival in China. We have hundreds of thousands of fiery young people pouring into the Kingdom who need to hear your story. They need to catch the Back to Jerusalem vision. God will use you to ignite within them a passion for China's role in the global harvest. All you need to do is simply tell your story. We need you—you must come!"

"God called me to go west, not to return eastward," he flatly announced. "I'm not going,"

At that, the Henan delegates got bulldog stubborn. "We're not going to leave you alone," they politely prodded him, "until you come with us."

When Simon saw that he would not have a moment's rest unless he relented, he realized he had little choice but to honor their wishes. The Lord confirmed to him that it was the right decision, so they bought a train ticket. They didn't have enough money to get him a sleeping berth or even a seat on the train, so he curled up on a newspaper on the floor, and thus made the four-day journey to Henan.

When he arrived, he was greeted like a war hero. Instantly in demand, he began to travel among the house churches, imparting a vision for global evangelization by the sheer force of his personal testimony and the power of the Spirit's anointing.

I can imagine the Lord thinking something like this back in 1948: "Simon Zhao, My servant, I love you! I love your passion, your consecration, your obedience, your devotion, your faith, and your abandonment to My purpose. And I want to call you to a higher place in Me. You will not understand the journey, but if you will hold tightly to My hand, I will bring you through and will multiply the effectiveness of your life beyond anything you could now imagine."

God could have let Simon cross the Chinese border, expend his life in some remote Asian village, and after a lifetime of labors have perhaps a dozen believers to present to His Lord. But instead, He chose to multiply Simon's life by giving him a story that would carry the authority of someone who had paid a steep price to gain his standing in God.

"I am taking you on a journey, Simon," I can suppose the Lord saying, "in which the vision that burns in your heart will be totally crushed. Your adversary will try to steal your faith and love. The losses in your life will be monumental. But My grace will preserve your heart, and in the end I will send you back into a fiery revival where your life will be multiplied many times over. Instead of touching just a few remote villages, you will ignite a flame in tens of thousands of fervent believers, and the impact of your life will be multiplied a thousand times over."

God does not call you to something and then change His mind.

When I learned of Simon's life on the internet,[3] his story ended with this Scripture: "For the gifts and the calling of God are irrevocable" (Romans 11:29). As I read that verse a fiery current shot through my spirit. YES! God does not call you to something and then change His mind. His call upon your life is still in force, even though you may be incarcerated in some kind of prison against your will. Even if you're buried in a veritable tomb, He is the God of resurrection. Never let go

---

[3] Visit www.backtojerusalem.com.

of your God! There is a day coming when you will witness the reality of Romans 11:29 because His calling over your life has not changed.

Simon Zhao finally died on December 7, 2001, but not before God had given him 13 years of fruitful ministry. (I find this reminiscent of Jacob, to whom God granted 17 years of vindication and honor at the end of his life.) Simon had no idea during those 40 years in prison that God was arranging a mighty revival in which he would share. How the adversary must have tried to discourage Simon from his faith! But he would not let go of his Savior.

No matter that he was a widower from whom the adversary had stolen 40 years. No matter that God had borne long with him. Simon continued to offer his love to his Lord, even when prayer was punished by torture, and the witness of his righteous life crashed thunderously on the shores of heaven. The God who loves justice rose up—in fury toward the adversary, in delight toward His afflicted one—and passed a sentence that would answer the demands of both restoration and restitution. And suddenly Simon found himself throwing gas upon the flames of possibly the greatest revival of the 20th century. His legacy will perpetuate in the lives of hundreds of spiritual children who will answer the call of the harvest.

"O you afflicted one, tossed with tempest, and not comforted, behold, I will lay your stones with colorful gems, and lay your foundations with sapphires. I will make your pinnacles of rubies, your gates of crystal, and all your walls of precious stones. All your children shall be taught by the LORD, and great shall be the peace of your children" (Isaiah 54:11-13).

O beloved, afflicted one, elect of God, your God is a God of justice. He hears your unrelenting prayers. He shall avenge you of your adversary. He will turn your barrenness to fruitfulness. Do not lose heart in prayer. Your calling and destiny is irrevocable!

"Nevertheless, when the Son of Man comes, will He really find faith on the earth?" (Luke 18:8).

You can't answer that question for anyone but yourself. When Jesus, after bearing long with you, comes to answer your prayer, will He find you growing in faith, leaning in love, praying always, gazing expectantly with uplifted, lovesick eyes?

God, give us an entire generation of Simon Zhaos! Give us an elect army that will not relent or lose heart in prayer, no matter what the adversary throws at them. Give us the true kind of faith, Lord, that perseveres all the way to breakthrough. By God's grace, we will stand in faith until we see "so great salvation" in our day and generation. Amen.

ORDER FORM

Books by Bob Sorge

	Qty.	Price	Total
BOOKS:			
MINUTE MEDITATIONS	_____	$12.00	_____
BETWEEN THE LINES:			
God is Writing Your Story	_____	$13.00	_____
OPENED FROM THE INSIDE	_____	$11.00	_____
IT'S NOT BUSINESS, IT'S PERSONAL	_____	$10.00	_____
POWER OF THE BLOOD	_____	$13.00	_____
UNRELENTING PRAYER	_____	$13.00	_____
LOYALTY: The Reach of the Noble Heart	_____	$14.00	_____
SECRETS OF THE SECRET PLACE	_____	$15.00	_____
Secrets of the Secret Place			
COMPANION STUDY GUIDE	_____	$11.00	_____
Secrets of the Secret Place DVD COURSE	_____	$30.00	_____
Secrets of the Secret Place LEADERS' MANUAL	_____	$ 5.00	_____
ENVY: The Enemy Within	_____	$12.00	_____
FOLLOWING THE RIVER: A Vision for			
Corporate Worship	_____	$10.00	_____
GLORY: When Heaven Invades Earth	_____	$10.00	_____
PAIN, PERPLEXITY & PROMOTION	_____	$14.00	_____
THE FIRE OF GOD'S LOVE	_____	$13.00	_____
THE FIRE OF DELAYED ANSWERS	_____	$14.00	_____
IN HIS FACE: A Prophetic Call to			
Renewed Focus	_____	$13.00	_____
EXPLORING WORSHIP: A Practical			
Guide to Praise & Worship	_____	$16.00	_____
Exploring Worship WORKBOOK &			
DISCUSSION GUIDE	_____	$ 5.00	_____
DEALING WITH THE REJECTION			
AND PRAISE OF MAN	_____	$10.00	_____

SPECIAL PACKET:

Buy one each of all Bob's books, and save 30%.
Call or visit our website for a current price.

Subtotal _____
Shipping Add 10% (Minimum of $4.50) _____
Missouri Residents Add 7.85% Sales Tax _____
Total Enclosed *(Domestic Orders Only/U.S. Funds)* _____

Send payment with order to: Oasis House
P.O. Box 522
Grandview, MO 64030-0522

Name _____

Address: Street _____

       City _____ State _____

       Zip _____ Email _____

For quantity discounts and MasterCard/VISA or international orders, call
816-767-8880 or order on our fully secure website: *www.oasishouse.com*.
See our site for free sermon downloads.